D1351594

EMMA V.I.P.

EMMA V.I.P.

by

SHEILA HOCKEN

LONDON
VICTOR GOLLANCZ LTD
1980

ISBN 0 575 02914 5

Published by arrangement with
Sphere Books Ltd.

Printed in Great Britain at
The Camelot Press Ltd, Southampton

*This book is dedicated to my husband, Don,
without whose complete faith and encouragement
I would never have written a word*

ILLUSTRATIONS

7

FOREWORD

MY FIRST BOOK, *Emma and I*, told the story of how my life as a blind person was utterly changed by the wisdom, cleverness, and affection of my guide-dog Emma, so much so that we became twin parts of one personality.

I was born in 1946 in Beeston, Nottingham. As a child, I could see a little but not enough to recognize people as more than vague images, or colours as blurred and muddy travesties of what I later learnt they really were. Both my brother Graham and I suffered from congenital cataracts which, in turn, caused retina damage. This was inherited from my father's side of the family. My mother had a different sort of eye complaint, caused by German measles when she was a child. All of us, therefore, were partially blind in varying degrees, although my father still managed to earn a living for us travelling round to markets selling drapery.

Eye surgery was not then as advanced as it is now, and an operation on Graham resulted in the total loss of the sight in one eye. I had also had an unsuccessful operation, but as a result of Graham's experience my parents decided against further attempts at surgery.

So when I started school, I could just see enough to be able to learn to read—if I held a book right up to my face—but the blackboard was a blur. In one respect concerning school, nevertheless, I was very lucky. My mother insisted that I should go to an ordinary school, and not a special one for the blind and visually handicapped, where willy-nilly I would have been taught braille despite my temporary ability to learn normal print. Her view was that such special schools, however well intentioned, kept blind children apart from the rest of the world—the sighted community—whereas what they most needed was to be integrated into it, and for this I have to thank her.

9

During my school career my sight gradually grew worse and by the time I was nineteen I was totally blind. I now had a job as a switchboard operator; when I had left school I badly wanted to work with animals (and despite not being able to see properly had helped at a local kennels at weekends) but it was somehow decreed that I should be a telephonist. So that is what I became, feeling over the switchboard to make the connections and taking notes on a braille machine. First I worked for a big dress shop in Nottingham, which was not a happy experience, and then, in a much more friendly atmosphere, for a firm called Industrial Pumps.

It was at this time that my life was made utterly different by the advent of Emma. I was, if the truth be known, ashamed of being blind. I refused to carry a white stick and hated asking for help. After all, I was a teenage girl, and I couldn't bear the idea that people would stare at me and think I was not like them. Partly as a result of this attitude I got lost one evening on the way home from work. I kept colliding with lamp-posts— and apologizing to them—and I couldn't find the bus stop, or hear anything that resembled a bus. I was nearly three hours late getting home, and it had been a frightening experience. But my Home Teacher was there when I arrived (Home Teachers visit the blind regularly to help and to supply aids such as braille paper, braille clocks, egg-timers that ring and so on) and after he had heard my story, he said: 'Why on earth don't you have a guide-dog?'

They were the nine most important words of my life. The result, eventually, was a spell at the Guide-Dog Training Centre at Leamington Spa—and Emma, the chocolate-brown Labrador who from the moment we met never wavered in her understanding and affection for me, and who never left my side. It was as if, suddenly, I had been supplied with an extra limb and an extra brain. Emma from then on guided me to work (and had her own ideas, often, about how she would get me there and back), saved my life—literally—and was intuitive to an unbelievable degree in realizing my needs, even to finding me a telephone-box when I desperately needed one in an area of Nottingham she had never been to before.

It was because of Emma that I finally found the courage to

go and share a flat in Nottingham with a girl, Anita, who became a marvellous friend. And at this time I met Don, who had a chiropody practice, whom I eventually married. With his love, care and attention added to that of Emma, I became doubly fortunate.

We moved into a little prefab bungalow; I got a new job with a big garage in the city, and I started going out with Emma and giving lectures and talks on Guide-Dogs. I also started (despite difficulties with sight invariably solved by Don) keeping, breeding, and showing Siamese cats which became, and has remained, a major interest.

Then came another event which transformed my life again. Mr Shearing, the specialist whom my brother Graham recommended me to go to, decided he would operate on me, although he warned that he did not work miracles.

To me, however, he *did* work a miracle. He gave me sight and, in September 1975, I saw the dazzling, unbelievable world for the first time with all its beauty and in all its incredible colour. For me, it was like being born again. I went home with Don and Emma and began life anew.

SHEILA HOCKEN

Stapleford
Nottinghamshire
April 1980

CHAPTER ONE

I LAY IN bed that night, unable to sleep, just thinking back over an incredible day. At the age of twenty-nine it had been my first day of life, real life that is: the day my husband Don had brought me home to Nottingham from hospital. Only a week before, and it now seemed a century ago, I had had the operation which had given me sight. But almost as soon as I had received that first unbelievable, incandescent shock of being able to see, the bandages had been replaced over my eyes. In the days that followed they were taken off again for only a minute or two and put back, so all the world I had seen was enclosed in the four walls of a hospital ward, and all I had caught sight of were glimpses, breathtaking and brief as they were, of the blues and greens of nurses' uniforms, and the yellows and crimsons of bowls of flowers on locker tops.

But today, today had been like no other since the Creation, too much, almost, for one human being. I lay there in bed and all its images tumbled and whirled through my mind like a laundromat machine gone mad: the sight of Don for the first time in my life—for I was quite blind when he married me—and the sensation in less than a second of all my imaginings of what he might be like being wiped away, and the reality approaching me up the ward being more handsome than ever I could have dreamt. The sight of my guide-dog Emma for the first time, the affectionate creature who had steered me through all sorts of difficulties, on whom I had relied and placed all my trust—but so much more beautiful than seemed possible. People had told me she was chocolate-coloured, and I had an idea of her appearance through feeling her coat and velvety ears, but no one had said she was a hundred different shades of brown, with a white patch on her chest, or that she was so bouncing with life and her eyes were so bright in the sunlight.

Then there had been that dazzling greenness that I could not make out until Don explained it to me. Grass! Something I had only felt through the soles of my shoes, something I knew existed, and that I dimly remembered from the days when, as a child, I could see a little. But that remembered grass, blurred and muddy green, now shone bright beyond belief, just as the entire world had become a landscape suddenly cleaned like an oil painting, and restored from beneath layers of thick, dead varnish.

These were major revelations, but there had been minor ones too: simply the delight of seeing water sparkle as it swirled from a tap, simply the sight of streets, shops, houses, and scores of people—something that when I was blind I somehow could never imagine, the idea of so many different lives going on around me but outside my own enclosed box of consciousness. And there had been strange shocks, including the sight of myself in a mirror. I felt as if I was looking at a stranger. I could not believe it was me. There had been disappointments as well, as when before teatime I had decided to be adventurous and go for the first time to the shops without Emma guiding me. I had taken her on a lead, and not on her usual guide-dog harness. But, once outside the gate and walking along, I had been terrified at the way lamp-posts and the trees and their shadows slanting across the pavement all seemed to rush at me, bearing down as if they were going to hit me. So I had shut my eyes, reverted instantly to blind ways, and had been thankful yet again for Emma who took over and even on a lead, guided me.

So the thoughts whirled round as I lay there. Beside me, Don was already asleep. But not only did I find sleep impossible, I did not want to drift off. It seemed such a waste of time spending eight hours with my eyes shut. Even though I could not see a thing in the dark, I just wanted to keep my eyes open. Somewhere lurking was the faint ghost of the feeling I had when in hospital they put the bandages back the first time, after I knew that, miraculously, I could see: what, I had thought then, if it's only a cruel joke and that's it? I knew it was irrational, but I felt that if I kept my eyes open all night then no one could take my sight away again.

Lying with my eyes open in the dark, I could not see anything. Yet this was not like being blind. The darkness of night is a different sort of darkness to blindness. People used to say, 'It must be terrible to live in the dark.' But over all those years going blind, and finally unable to see at all, it was not like living in the dark, because light and dark are opposites and if you don't have one—that is, light—then you don't know what darkness is. Only when you can see can you understand that you were living in the dark in a different sense. So it was with me lying there that first night at home, and I realized that blindness is not a black dark like night. It is a sort of void darkness, a non-colour darkness, an indescribable sort of limbo, neither black nor grey, nor brown, nor any visual colour, and lying awake and seeing nothing was exciting because this was the black of true night that I had never known before.

But if that was a new sensation experienced in the night, also through my mind went the countless new sensations of that day apart from visual experience. It was as if all sorts of other things had suddenly come alive as well as my sight—ambitions, hopes for the future, and bodily things. I was aware of blood racing round my veins, my heart beating, lots of other things I had never thought existed before. I suppose it was because I felt more alive than I had ever done before, and visual sensation stimulates the rest of your body. As a blind person, things can be very exciting and you enjoy life—but there is so much more when you have a visual stimulant.

More materially, I thought, What about driving a car? Wouldn't that be great! Could I read? Apart from trying to identify the word SALT on a box in the food cupboard, and the names of cereals, I hadn't yet even looked at print. I had been so excited with all the fabulous colours I had seen I had not really stopped to think whether I could read or not, or how much I had retained from my early partially-sighted days at school.

I heard Emma snoring and I looked over and knew that, unseen, there was the shape of a dark, curled-up ball of fur and affection at the bottom of our bed. Then, suddenly, I had an awful thought. What about Emma?

I sat up in bed. I was horrified.

'What about Emma?' I found myself shouting aloud.

Don grumbled a bit and turned over. 'I won't need her any

more as a guide-dog. Will they take her away?' I started to shake Don. 'Don, wake up, wake up—what about Emma?' I said again.

'What's the matter with Emma?' he said sleepily. 'She's all right, isn't she?'

I felt him moving his foot about to feel her at the end of the bed.

'Yes, of course she's all right, but I don't need her any more as a guide-dog.'

'Well, of course you don't. Isn't it marvellous?' He turned over to go to sleep again.

'But they might take her away from me.'

At that, Don sat up.

'Who might?'

'The people at Guide-Dogs.'

'Oh never. They won't. Don't worry about it. Try and go to sleep.'

'But they might.'

'She's nearly eleven,' said Don. 'Who'd want to have her at that age? Nobody else could use her as a guide-dog.'

'Yes, I know,' I said. 'But they do have the *right* to take her away from me if I don't need her any more.'

'Oh, they wouldn't. Believe me, petal, they won't take her away from you. Don't be silly.'

I realized it was no good discussing it with Don. I lay back, still with my eyes open, and the worry grew and, like a growing storm cloud, blotted out the memory of the wonderful day. I could not bear the thought of living without Emma. What would I do? I know, I won't tell them, I thought. I won't tell them at Guide-Dogs that I can see. But no, that would be silly, they'd be bound to find out and then what? They surely wouldn't, they *couldn't*. I wouldn't let them take her away, they'd have to shoot me first. I put my hand down and stroked Emma's head; she was still snoring and occasionally twitching and giving little growls in her sleep. Dreaming, but all unaware that life had changed. I whispered, 'They won't take you back, Emma. I won't let them.'

I lay back again, and, with determination in my mind, I eventually got to sleep.

I woke up to see our pink wallpaper, and the sun shining through the window. For a moment I forgot about worrying whether they would take Emma away or not, because the wonderful, unaccustomed daylight had taken over again.

There was so much to do, so much to see, so much to plan. I got out of bed and went to the front door. There was the *Daily Express* sticking through the letter-box. Print! Could I read? I pulled the paper out and looked at the headlines. I could see them perfectly well. But what did they mean? I couldn't make any sense of the great black letters. I kept looking, and it was like looking at double-Dutch, or what I assumed people meant by double-Dutch. I put the paper down thinking, Well, it was too much to expect. Don came out of the bedroom.

'I thought I might be able to read the paper,' I said, 'but it doesn't seem to make a lot of sense.'

'But you used to read when you were little, didn't you?'

'Oh yes, I learnt to read, but it's a long time ago.' So long it could be a different person, and there was an instant memory of the small edition of that person, aged about eight, at her desk in school, knowing that other girls and boys somehow had an easier time of things and that she had to put her face right up to a book to learn to read, but fortunately not knowing that within a very few years even doing that would not enable her to see print. To the right she could vaguely see the shape of Trudy, the little girl who sat next to her, holding her book on her desk. Trudy was giggling and saying, 'What are you smelling your book for, Sheila?'

'I'm not smelling it, I'm reading it.'

More giggles.

'You're silly,' Trudy said, stretching her arms right out as she held her book. 'I can read my book like this.'

All little Sheila had done then was to hold her book away as well, but the print immediately blurred and went out of focus so that she had to bring it back to her face to restore the Cat to the Mat, and reassure herself. When she had done that she had just observed rather lamely, 'I'm *not* silly.'

The mental images and sounds of the classroom were dissolved by Don's voice. 'Don't forget,' he was saying, 'you haven't got your lenses yet. You'll want glasses before you can read.'

'I never thought about that,' I said. But, of course, had I thought about it, I would have realized immediately. My blindness had been caused by congenital cataracts inherited from my father's side of the family. My brother Graham suffered the same defect as I, and my mother had a different sort of eye complaint caused by German measles. We were a family all blind in varying degrees and I should have remembered the importance of glasses which, in our little circle, were just about as vital as breathing itself. The cataract operation I'd had takes the lens part of the eye away so that focusing, especially close up, is not possible without glasses or contact lenses.

'I suppose I'll want reading glasses,' I said. Then a thought struck me. 'My Dad's got a pair—big thick ones. If I could borrow them, I could probably focus on the print better, and it wouldn't take me long to remember all the words. . . . Don, let's go and see him today.'

'Well, why not?' said Don, though in his voice there was the hint that this might bring disappointment. 'Shall we have breakfast first though?'

I had forgotten this important part of the beginning of the day, and was a bit dashed because I wanted to rush out to the car there and then to fetch the lenses from my father. It was strange cooking breakfast—or at least attempting to. Even stranger, it might seem, that I found it harder than cooking when I was blind. I had managed quite happily then, judging everything by feel and taste, and with the aid of a braille regulo on my cooker. But this was so different. Quite apart from being unable to co-ordinate my movements and judge distances accurately as sighted people do automatically (I got the frying-pan a bit to the right of the hot-plate at first, and an inch or so above it) it meant nothing to me to actually see bacon fat turning to crispy gold and the transparency of an egg gradually becoming white.

'When's bacon cooked?' I said to Don. 'And eggs?'

'What do you mean, petal?'

'Well, I used to be able to judge by feel . . . with a fork . . . bacon, anyway, and I just used to sort of time the egg.'

'Yes, I know,' he said. 'You either got them half done or so hard I couldn't get my bread anywhere near them.' He smiled. I knew he was joking.

'Isn't it lovely to look at somebody and see them smiling,' I said. 'I'd have thought you were serious if you'd said that to me last week.' That quite perked me up. Yesterday had shown so many marvellous things about sight. Today had brought some problems, but here was something else I had found out. 'Now, Don,' I said in a tone of mock severity, 'how do you know when bacon's done?'

He laughed. 'When it looks done,' he said.

'Yes, I know *that*. But what does "looks done" *mean*?'

He became serious. 'Well, it's a bit difficult to explain. Why don't you test it as you used to and then you can see what it looks like, and then you'll be able to judge by eye.'

Tentatively I put a fork into the rashers, and it didn't *feel* cooked.

'It's not cooked yet,' I said.

Don stood over me at the stove, and explained. 'No, you can see it's still too pink there. It needs to go a darker shade yet— more *cooked* looking.'

I had to laugh. 'It's no good you standing there and saying "more cooked-looking"! I'm trying to learn what it means.'

Finally, somehow, and with the aid of my old, familiar methods, the breakfast was cooked. Emma came trotting into the dining-room as we carried the plates in, and as Don sat down she did as well, just by his chair, with her nose pointed up towards his breakfast. I looked at her.

'Does she always do that?' I asked.

'Didn't you know? She always sits near me in case I drop a crumb or two.'

'Oh yes,' I said, not utterly convinced. I went on with my breakfast. 'You don't give her titbits, do you? You know the rules about titbits.'

Don looked up, slightly guiltily, I thought, with a piece of bacon poised on his fork.

'Certainly not.'

But the expression on his face told me he was not quite telling the truth, and this notion was reinforced by the very expectant look on Emma's face. Sight had brought yet another revelation of things as they really were!

But at the time I did not dwell on this. Emma sitting there, nose quivering, eyes all bright and eager, and with her tail giving tentative little wags at the mention of her name had reminded me of the thoughts of the previous night, and the whole terrible prospect of losing Emma came back with a rush.

'Oh . . . Emma!' I said.

'What's the matter?'

'You remember what I said last night? They might want her back.'

Don looked at me steadfastly across the breakfast table. 'Sheila, you mustn't worry like this. Of course they won't want her back. She's your dog, she's nearly eleven, she'd be retiring anyway soon, wouldn't she? And you'd have kept her then, wouldn't you?'

'Well, yes, I know. But I can't remember anything like this happening before. I can't remember hearing of a guide-dog owner getting their sight back.'

'Look,' said Don, 'the best thing is to ring them. Don't sit worrying about it. Give them a ring, now.'

'I can't,' I said.

'Why not?'

'It's Saturday. There won't be anyone at the office. I'll have to wait till Monday. Oh dear.' The worry crowded in on me. I patted Emma on the head and she wagged her tail as if to reassure me. Monday seemed an age away.

'Come on,' said Don. He got up from the table, came round and put an arm round me. 'Don't worry. Let's go and get those lenses from your Dad.'

We all got into the car, and I turned and looked round at Emma who had jumped into the back seat. It was so lovely just to be able to turn and look at her. But immediately I visualized one of the guide-dog trainers coming to take her away. I shut my eyes and made the picture go away, and opened them again and looked out of the front window of the car. We were driving into Nottingham.

'Isn't there a lot of traffic?' I said. 'I suppose I did think of other cars on the road when I couldn't see because I heard them, but you don't hear all of them because of your own engine noise. It cuts a lot of sound out.' Being in a car used to be rather strange because I never formed a picture of the outside world at all. Then suddenly I said, 'Will you teach me to drive?'

Don looked at me. 'Well, if you want me to. But you have to have good eyesight to drive you know.'

'Yes,' I said, 'I know.'

'I mean, you've got to be able to read a number-plate at twenty-five yards.'

'Well I can certainly do that,' I said. 'I can see the trees, and all those leaves on the pavement. . . .'

'All right then. See that white car . . . what's the number-plate?'

I screwed my eyes up. What white car? Where? 'Which car?' I said.

'The one up in front. It's about twenty-five yards away.'

'Ah, I've got it.'

'What does the number-plate say?'

'Mm, no, I can't make it out. Can you go a bit closer.'

Don drove a bit closer. He laughed. 'Any nearer and we'll be touching. Can you see the number-plate?'

'Ah . . . no.'

Don made a wry sort of face. 'Well, petal, don't rush things. It doesn't matter.'

So I gave up trying to find the number-plate, let alone decipher what it said. Obviously driving a car was something for the future. Not exactly a disappointment, because Don was quite right. I was expecting too much, too soon, perhaps.

Having borrowed the lenses from my father, Don and I went straight back home. I couldn't wait to know if I could read. As soon as I got in, I put the special glasses on and picked up the paper again. There was an immediate improvement. 'Don,' I called, 'come here. I can see all the letters.' It was true. The trouble was I couldn't remember which was which.

'What's that one? Is that a P or an R?' Don patiently identified them for me, in turn, and at last it all began to make a little sense. 'It *is* coming back,' I said, 'P-L-A-C-E . . . place—that's what it says, isn't it?'

'Yes, that's right,' said Don, 'and what's that one?'

'I-N—yes, in! Gosh, isn't it fantastic.'

I didn't speak for minutes after that, and Don left me to it. I simply buried my face in the paper and read every word I could find. But there were quite a lot of words I simply could not make head nor tail of. Not for some time after that morning did I realize that I suffer from a kind of word blindness. I suppose it was because I hadn't read anything but braille for years and my brain didn't act very quickly when I saw proper print. Instead of looking at a line and being able to read it off as any other literate sighted person would, I had to go through each word, letter by letter, before it made sense. Things have improved since then, but I still suffer to an extent from this 'word blindness' and I am a very slow reader. Not that it takes any of my enjoyment out of reading—I might take ages and ages to read a book but it is still one of my great pleasures, and since that day I have never had to use braille again in earnest.

Don came back after I had been sitting with the newspaper for, it seemed, hours. 'Do you want me to take you to the shops to get something for lunch? Then we can go out into the country and look at the fields.'

'No, I don't think so, Don,' I said. 'I think I'll walk. I've got to get used to it.' I was remembering the horrifying experience I had had the day before when I had gone out for the first time with Emma. Yet I knew I had to get used to going out and, although it had proved a frightening experience, it had been curiously exciting and thrilling as well. I wanted to have another try, to see how the pavement and lamp-posts and hedges behaved this time—and I also wanted another look in the shops.

'Are you going to take Emma?' said Don.

'Oh I won't go without Emma. I won't use a harness, though. I'll just put her lead on. I'll take it slowly, and make sure no hedges get me on the way!'

I went out of the door, and again had that uncanny feeling of the ground moving beneath me and the gate coming towards me. Then when I got to the gate—or it got to me—I couldn't find the latch. I could see it perfectly well but I just couldn't locate it with my hand. Lack of co-ordination again. So I shut my eyes and felt—it was much easier. For quite a time looking at things just put me off altogether and I had to go back to my old ways.

I decided we would go to the paper-shop first as I wanted to buy some women's magazines.

'Come on, Emma, we'll go to the paper-shop. I'm going to buy a magazine. Isn't it exciting!' She looked up at me, not quite sure what I was talking about, and still not understanding why she had no harness on. She tried to keep the same pace in front of me as she had always done and she stopped as usual at the kerbs. When we arrived, and on the mention of 'paper-shop', she turned in, as she would have done if she had been leading me.

I looked at the counter full of papers and magazines. Which one should I buy? I went for the brightest of all the brightly-coloured covers—a woman about my age modelling a stunning dress in green against a pink background. As I was deciding, Mrs Hill, who kept the shop, finished with another customer and came over to me.

'Hello, Sheila, how nice to see you. I heard the news about your operation. It's marvellous!'

'Yes, isn't it?'

Then she saw Emma, and said, 'Oh . . . no harness today.'

'No, isn't it lovely? She can go on a lead and have all the walks she wants now.' Emma lay by the counter, head between her paws and looking up with an expression which seemed to say: 'Well, I'm not sure about all this; I'll believe it when it happens.'

But Mrs Hill looked a bit perplexed. 'Doesn't that mean they'll take her back to Guide-Dogs, though, now you don't need her?'

Don't need her? I thought. How can people think that way? All the anxieties were started up again and I wanted to get out of the shop with Emma immediately, even though I knew Mrs Hill was only anxious on my behalf and meant no harm.

'I really don't know, I'm afraid,' I said. 'I'm going to ring the Guide-Dog people first thing on Monday and find out. But I'm sure they won't take her away.' And, going out of the door, I added for bravado, 'I won't let them, anyway.' Mrs Hill's expression didn't seem very hopeful as I said this, but at least Emma gave an approving wag as we left the shop.

The next day we went for a drive into the Nottinghamshire countryside. We parked down a lane and set off across the fields. Emma ran on in front, tail in the air, stopping every so often to snuffle in the grass and enjoy the new scents, while Don and I, who somehow had set off separately, kept calling to one another to come and look at this flower, or that. Then, suddenly, having been walking quite happily, I found myself falling: rolling, rolling down somewhere. Luckily it could not have been very far, because when I landed at the bottom I was still in one piece. I sat up. Don came running.

'Are you all right?'

'Yes. What happened?' I said.

'There's a grassy bank there, didn't you see it?'

'No. What grassy bank?' I looked back. It all looked just level grass to me.

Don helped me to my feet, 'Come on, walk up and down it.'

Holding his hand, I put my feet out gingerly. Yes, the ground *did* go up steeply. I walked up with him and then, on my own, down again. But however much I walked up and down the bank, I could not actually *see* the incline. It was rather disturbing. I could get the idea much better if I closed my eyes than I could by looking at it.

'You'll have to be careful,' said Don, 'at least until you can weigh up this sort of thing.'

It is strange how vision gives you the distance and depth of things, but that information has to be processed, as in a computer, by the mind. This process of assessment comes with experience, and to someone like me had to be learned. It was another odd revelation. I had expected that when I could see I would be able to see everything, immediately. I had not imagined I would be unable to judge how high a step was, or that the ground inclined one way or the other.

'It was a lot safer with Emma,' I called to Don when we had resumed our walk.

'Well, take my arm.'

'No, I'd rather not,' I said. I was not ungrateful but I knew

24

I had to learn on my own. 'But you can shout if you think I'm going to walk into anything. . . . I can't go back to having Emma on harness again, can I?'

At the mention of her name, Emma, who was a few yards ahead, looked up. She had obviously found something interesting at the bottom of a tree and had started digging a hole. Then I saw her throw herself up in the air and roll on the floor.

'Emma!' I heard Don shout, 'NO!'

I stood there in amazement. 'What's the matter? What's she doing?'

He rushed up to her, grabbed her by the collar and started to drag her away from the tree.

'Oh dear. It's not too bad,' he said. 'Have you brought any paper hankies?'

I delved in my handbag and gave him a wad of tissues. 'What's the matter? What did she do? Has she hurt herself?'

Then Don started laughing. 'No, nothing like that. Come and have a look.'

I looked, and saw—but not only saw when I got closer—what had happened.

Emma's coat was a subtly different shade of brown. But there was nothing subtle about her aroma. She had found a cow-pat and rolled in it.

'I think we can get most of it off,' said Don.

'Oh, *that's* what she was doing when she was rolling.'

'Yes. Don't you remember that picnic we went on and she did the same thing?'

I remembered all too well. Just after we had first met, Don had taken me on a picnic in Charnwood Forest and Emma had covered herself, but not in glory, and I had then discovered to my relief that Don is a kind and tolerant man.

Then, as now, it had been impossible not to be very conscious of Emma in the back of the car, with the exception that on this occasion I could actually see how unlike her usual, well-trained guide-dog self she looked. At the same time I thought: I don't care if she does roll in cow-pats and smells like a farmyard. I still love her. And as we drove back, what Monday had in store for that bedraggled, and now sleeping, figure on the back seat seemed an unbearably long way away.

CHAPTER TWO

MONDAY BROUGHT A bright, hazy, autumnal morning; but it was not as autumnal as I was feeling inside. I was tight with anxiety, and all sorts of other feelings had started when Emma had got out of her basket, stretched, and looked up at me with those lovely, eager eyes, and I patted her, said ''Morning, Emma,' and felt a lump in my throat.

'Shall I dial the number for you?' asked Don. He understood, although neither of us had mentioned the matter, that I needed encouragement and was trying to put off the actual moment of ringing Guide-Dogs.

'No, I'll do it,' I said, putting on a brave face, which I knew, by Don's look, had not taken him in for a moment. 'You go and read the paper.'

'All right, petal.' He smiled and patted my arm, then went off into the other room with the paper.

I went to the phone and looked at it for a moment. It was no good putting it off. I picked up the receiver and started dialling.

They answered almost immediately, and so quickly that I heard the girl say, 'Guide-Dogs for the Blind . . .' And then again, slightly impatiently when I said nothing, 'Guide-Dogs for the Blind . . .' I thought: I could put the phone down now. Her voice somehow sounded like an invitation to a turning in my life I did not want to take.

But I said, 'Can I speak to Mr Wright, please?'

There was a pause and some clicks, and then I heard Mr Wright. Again I had the impulse to abandon the whole idea, to run away, to collect Emma and disappear and not tell them anything. But, in a voice that did not seem to belong to me, I heard myself saying: 'Sheila Hocken speaking . . .' and felt my heart thumping as he replied.

'Oh Mrs Hocken. Good morning. Let's see . . . Emma, isn't it?'

No going back now.

'Er . . . yes.'

'Well, what can we do for you?'

'Er . . . well, she's getting on . . . she's nearly eleven . . .' It was not what I had meant to say. The words hung there in the wires for a moment, because I still could not bring myself to the point. My hand was trembling and I reached with the other for my cigarettes.

Distantly, and with an ominously brisk and business-like overtone, or so it seemed, Mr Wright replied: 'You're worried about her age?'

'Mm . . . yes and no . . . I thought . . . I'd just tell you. She's due for retirement fairly soon, I suppose.'

'Well, I'd better have a look at her file.' There was a pause and I lit another cigarette, having stubbed the previous one halfway down. I heard him pick up his receiver again.

'She was working very well on our last report. I'm sure there's no question of her retiring yet awhile.'

I decided it was no good beating about the bush.

'Mr Wright . . . it's not just her age I want to tell you about. I've just had an operation on my eyes . . . and I can see now. . . .'

It all came out in a rush, and there really was no going back now.

'How absolutely marvellous,' said the voice at the other end, somehow unexpectedly delighted. 'Congratulations. That really is wonderful—'

But I am afraid I cut off his congratulations.

'Yes, it's unbelievable,' I said. 'But what about Emma?'

There was a silence, then a tone of slight surprise.

'I don't quite follow . . . what *about* Emma?'

'Well, I don't need to use her as a guide-dog any more. I thought . . . you'll want her back—you're not having her, you know.'

There was another silence from the other end, and then, while I stubbed out my cigarette and wanted to hang up without hearing what he had to say, there was a laugh from Mr Wright.

'Whatever gave you that idea, Mrs Hocken? Of course we

shan't want Emma back. She's *your* dog. She can retire, and you can take *her* for walks instead of the other way round.'

I didn't say anything for a moment, and once again my eyes could not see—but only because they were full of tears.

I heard Mr Wright saying, 'Mrs Hocken . . . are you there?'

'Yes,' I said faintly.

'Now,' he said consolingly, 'it really wouldn't be fair to take Emma from you, would it? We don't do that, you know. You go and enjoy yourself. . . . I'm going straight away to cross Emma off our list. And congratulations again. It's wonderful.'

Wonderful! It certainly was. Mr Wright was talking about my sight, but I was thinking about Emma. Don came out of the other room and didn't even say 'I told you so.' We said nothing, just hugged in this huge and marvellous relief. And while we stood there embracing, I felt a cold nose on my leg and heard the swish of a tail. Emma looked up at us both, eyes bright, wagging her tail furiously.

She knew, too.

Later that day there was a telephone call from George Miller, the blind newspaper reporter through whom I had originally met Don. He had heard about my operation and wanted to put a story in the local paper.

'I'd rather you didn't,' I said.

'Oh, come on, Sheila, it's a great bit of news. Let me use it.'

'George, I promise I will let you use it, but not just yet.'

'Well, why not?'

To be honest, I really couldn't say why not. I think possibly I was a little worried. There was so much I had suddenly gained, and I didn't want to lose it. I think I was afraid that if I made it public, perhaps it would go. Everything was so precious and perhaps it was a silly idea on my part, but I promised George that if he gave me three months I would come back to him, and then he could put a story in the local paper.

In the event, the three months did not elapse. He rang up again a week or two later and persuaded us to go on his Radio Nottingham programme, and not long after that he came round to visit us and discuss the programme.

It was marvellous to see him. I had known him for ten years, but had never actually *seen* him before. And—as I came to realize more and more—as with other people I had known only by their voices and general sense of presence, he was so different from how I had imagined him. The only way I can explain this is to compare how someone you have known as a radio voice can sometimes be totally and wildly different if you see them on television. It was like this with George, only more so. I had guessed that he was not very tall and rather plump. But before I really had time to notice how different he was from my original image of him, I had a shock.

It was so patently obvious by looking at George that he could not see: something about the eyes and the expression on the face. That was a deep shock because I had heard people say that you could always tell if someone was blind, but I had never really believed them. 'How *could* they know?' I had always asked myself. 'We may be blind, but we have eyes and the same features as anyone else.' I would never accept the idea and it was a quite horrible thought to me. But then, at the moment of looking at George for the first time, there was the proof, both upsetting and inescapable. It really was obvious that he just could not see.

Don followed George through the door. 'Are you all right, old lad?' he said. 'Let me take your coat.'

I realized then that I was just standing there, staring at him. 'Sorry George,' I said. 'Let me take your coat.' I took it from him and went to hang it up.

'I'll get you a drink, George,' Don said. 'What'll you have?'

'Oh, a glass of beer'll do me,' he said.

I was still looking at him, fascinated, but realized I ought to do something. 'Come and sit down, George,' I said.

I didn't want to grab him and drag him to a chair; I wanted to make it least embarrassing for him, just as I would have wanted it to be when I was blind. I said, 'This way, George.' And he followed my voice.

'It's to the right of the door, just round the back. That's right.' I saw him feeling for the seat, and then turn round and sit on it.

'Well, now then, kid, how are you keeping?' George always called me that. He always regarded me as his kid sister.

29

'Oh, I'm fine, George. On top of the world.'

'You'll do this programme, you and Don?'

'We'd love to.'

'Great stuff, great stuff, kid.'

Exactly ten years before, George had started a programme on Radio Nottingham for blind people, called Wednesday Club. I had been on the very first programme, in those dark days, so many years ago, and for his tenth anniversary of first going on the air he wanted me on again, even though I was no longer in the blind community.

'You'll come on as well, won't you, Don?' he said as he heard Don come in from the kitchen with a glass of beer.

'Oh, I will George, I said I would.'

'Great stuff, lad.'

'Here's your beer, George, on the table.'

I watched as George felt for the table edge and then felt round for his glass of beer.

'Cheers!' George turned towards me but he didn't actually look at me. 'Where's my Emma?' he said, putting his glass down.

'She's in front of you, George.'

'Come on, my old girl, let's have a fuss.' George put his hand down, and Emma instinctively moved towards him and snuffled her nose into his hand, wagging her tail furiously.

'Now then, old girl. How are you? You're having an easy life of it these days, aren't you?'

'George, watch out! Ming's just about to get on your back.'

'Glad you warned me,' he said as Ming, one of my Siamese cats, landed on his shoulders. Animals seemed to collect round George like bees round the honeypot, perhaps because they instinctively knew he could not see and sought bodily contact. I don't know why it was, but it seems to happen with blind people, certainly as far as my animals are concerned.

'Well,' said George, untroubled by Ming's attentions and still stroking Emma, 'what's it like being in the visual world?' His voice was quite matter-of-fact. He might have been discussing the football results. There was not a hint of envy in the question, just mild curiosity.

I didn't know how to reply, but I said, 'George, it's marvellous, absolutely fantastic. I don't know how to describe it.'

Only then did George seem to look away from me with the shadow of a wistful expression passing over his face, as if he was on the other side of a gulf from me. It made me feel terrible. How could I really say what it was like?

'Try and tell me, kid,' George said. 'It would be nice to hear from somebody like you.' I thought that was very brave, and also sad, and I still could not say anything because coming from me, who knew what it was like to be blind, a description of the world he could never know would, I am certain, have been upsetting in a way a sighted person's description could never be.

So all I said was: 'Well, George, it's marvellous. Sitting here and looking at everything in the room. Just that.' And even then I thought I might have said too much for him. Then Don stepped in and rescued me.

'You haven't seen the kitchen since we did it up, have you?' he said.

'Oh, that's a coincidence,' said George. 'I'm having my kitchen done. Let's have a look round and see if you've got any new ideas.'

A 'look round' to George, and any other blind person, really means a feel, or, as we call it in the blind world, a 'fleck'. As I used to call it, that is.

I went with them into the kitchen and saw George feeling round walls and cupboards and windows. When he got to the back door, his hands touched our new louvre window.

'What's this, what's this, Don?' he asked, excitedly feeling all the different layers of glass.

'It's a louvre window,' said Don. 'It's really handy for ventilation. You ought to have one. Feel down this side. Look, feel the handles.'

George felt along the side of the door, felt the handles and experimentally pulled and pushed them to make the windows open and close.

'Fantastic,' he said finally. 'I've never seen one of these before.'

When you cannot see, things such as this are all about you but you are not aware of them. And there are so many things immediately around that even the most attentive sighted person cannot tell you about everything. To a sighted person a mere

31

glance interprets everything about something like a louvre window, but to a blind person it has to be explained: its function —how it lets the condensation out, but doesn't let the cold air in—and how it works in general and can be adjusted to suit different conditions. Blind people not only want to know that, but they also want to know how it feels when it's open, when it's closed and when it's half closed—something that a sighted person can assimilate in two seconds just by looking.

When we came out of the kitchen George still seemed in no hurry to talk about his forthcoming programme. Instead we sat and chatted.

'Do you remember those days when you used to ring me, our kid?' he said.

'I do, George.'

'We had some good times.' He chuckled, and took another pull of his beer. 'Do you remember the Opticon?'

The Opticon? I thought. Then it came back, just as George sensed in the brief silence that I had not remembered.

'I was going to buy you one, Sheila, don't you remember?' Don said.

'Of course,' I said. 'The tactile reading machine.'

'That's it.'

'Have you got one yet, George?'

He laughed. 'No . . . I'm still saving!'

'Are they still as expensive?'

'About two thousand quid.'

I remembered the night that George had rung me, about six months before the operation. He had been so excited. 'Listen, Sheila . . . I've got this terrific news. There's an incredible machine just been invented by an American. It's called the Opticon. It translates all the visual images into tactile images that you can feel. You can read *anything* with it. Can you imagine. . . ?' I had, in an instant, been able to imagine and realized the new, undreamt-of possibilities for blind people, George and myself included. In an instant I had become as excited as he was.

'Oh, George! Where can we get one from? What do we do?'

'Ah. It's not as simple as that.' He calmed down a bit and told me about the enormous cost of the machines. They were only in the experimental stage, and there were only one or two in Britain.

All very dampening, of course. But the basic idea remained: a marvellous new machine that could alter the life of any blind person. When Don came in that evening I had told him, pouring out enthusiasm to him just as George had to me over the telephone. Don listened and said immediately, and with no more deliberation than if he had been about to order a pound of tea, 'We'll have one!'

'But Don,' I said, 'where are we going to get two thousand pounds from?'

'Never mind the money.'

'And don't forget the operation,' I said. By now I had become cautious, and vaguely wondered if Don was thinking of rushing out and robbing a bank.

'Ah, the operation . . . yes,' said Don thoughtfully. 'Well, I suppose we ought to wait to see how it goes.' He had always been reluctant to discuss what might happen if I got sight. And even more, if the operation did not prove a success. So the subject was dropped. But later that evening Don suddenly said, 'I tell you what. If the operation's a success, I'll buy you a colour TV. And if not I'll buy you an Opticon.'

George brought back the entire memory of that evening, sitting there in the same room where those words had been spoken and those promises made—and sitting, now, next to a new colour television set!

When, finally, we had discussed details of the Radio Nottingham programme and George had gone, I reflected with shame that in the presence of blind people I was uneasy. I still am. Not because I do not know what to do or that I am afraid of blindness, like an ordinary sighted person, but it makes me feel guilty: guilty that I have sight while people like George have not. I think constantly of all those other friends who are still left behind on the other side of that dark wall. And my shouting to them and telling them how wonderful it is on this side does not relieve the guilt nor, more importantly, do them any good.

The Radio Nottingham programme duly went out and George had a story printed in the local paper, and from that moment things began to happen. One of the very first exciting things was that Robin Brightwell of the BBC 2 *Horizon* programme rang me.

'I'm producing a programme,' he told me, 'about blind people, but mainly blind children, and I thought it would be a good idea to have you, maybe at the beginning of the programme, to say what it's like to have your sight restored and make a really good opening. How do you feel about it?'

I was thrilled and flattered and agreed immediately, but I said, 'You'll want Emma in as well, won't you?'

'Oh, well, yes, of course,' he said, after some hesitation.

So it was arranged that he would come up and see us on a Sunday in January so that we could discuss the filming arrangements. I remember that Sunday so vividly because, apart from anything else, it started to snow. 'It's snowing!' Don had called out, and I had immediately rushed into the garden. It was so beautiful, and something else I had never seen before. I watched the white flakes floating down from the sky and landing on my coat, stopping for a while, and then slowly melting away.

'What are you up to out there?' Don shouted from the kitchen window.

'I'm watching the snow. Isn't it incredible?'

'Well, if you say so,' he laughed. 'But it's a lot nicer from in here. You'll freeze.'

'No,' I said. 'It's so lovely out here, and I can't feel the cold.' I felt I wanted to stay there all day, holding my head up to the sky which was whirling with snowflakes, drifting and swirling down. I saw that when they reached the grass they alighted so gently, as if someone was putting them there one by one. It wasn't at all like rain, which is very aggressive. It was as if each had wings.

Eventually I went inside to wait for Robin Brightwell to arrive, but I made sure that I was always able to see out of a window and watch the snowflakes. I noticed that as the snow began to settle and everything turned white, it all seemed to look brighter and cleaner and there were new reflections inside the house. This might appear very ordinary and unremarkable to anyone used to the sight of snow, but it was an astonishing revelation to me.

34

Robin Brightwell was just how I expected a television producer to be: tall, dark, with a beard, and intelligent-looking. We sat and discussed the programme.

'We'd like to come down on Tuesday, if that's all right with you,' he said.

'Yes, fine. What have you got in mind for the filming?'

'Well, I think we'd like to film you on a railway station, and possibly in a local shop. I remember you saying on the broadcast that often you can't relate to objects: you're able to see an object, but not able to identify what it actually is until you've touched it. Perhaps we might be able to put that idea over on film.'

'There's a little shop round the corner,' I told him, 'which would do very well for that. It's a hardware shop and has lots and lots of different things in it, and some of them I *know* I can't identify.' We laughed, and when Robin had walked round the corner with me and seen the shop he agreed that it would be just the place.

The following Tuesday the production team were due at 8.30 am.

'What shall I wear?' I said to Don. 'What do you think I look slimmest in?' Once I was able to see, I had been able to judge my figure against other women's, and I had had to admit to myself that I could do with being a bit slimmer. I had also learnt that different colours could alter how slim or otherwise you looked.

'I think you ought to wear your navy-blue dress,' said Don.

'Right,' I said. 'That does make me look a bit slimmer.'

As I said that I realized once again how, in all sorts of unpredictable ways, my world and a whole lot of attitudes had changed with vision. Before, I think I would have chosen something that I felt comfortable in, something made of material of which I liked the feel. Now those considerations no longer came into it. No matter how uncomfortable I might feel, I had to look my best. I don't know which value is right, but I do know that visual judgements had by now completely taken over the way I dressed.

When 8.30 came and the bell rang at the front door I expected Robin and possibly two or three other people, but

35

I was not prepared for the army assembled on my doorstep! Robin came in, followed by someone else, followed by someone else and so on, until a crowd of football-match proportions was inside the house. Robin introduced them all: the assistant producer, the cameraman, the photographer, the sound man . . . and so on.

'Do you mean to tell me that it takes *all* of you to make a film?' I asked.

'Well,' said Robin, 'it does—but we're really short-staffed.' He sounded a little put out.

Then started the very gruelling, down-to-earth business of making a film. After that day I knew I never wanted to be a film star—not that I would ever have the opportunity. I had never before realized what a tedious and boring business film-making is.

'We've fixed up to film at the local station, with British Rail's co-operation,' said Robin. 'We want to film you buying a ticket and then, on the train, what you're looking at out of the window. We'll do the wild tracks later.'

'Wild tracks?' I asked. 'What are those?'

'Oh, soundtracks that you fit to the film afterwards.'

Off we went to the station, and Robin told me that if I saw anything I was not quite sure about or obstacles that I did not recognize immediately, I was to tell him. This was because at that time I was still very much learning to translate the identity of objects into my mind through sight alone. When we got on to the platform I saw some red things hanging on a wall and told him about them.

'Fire-buckets,' he said. 'Haven't you come across those before?'

'No, I haven't been on many trains, I must admit,' I said. 'At least, not since I've been able to see.'

We went to the ticket office, Emma trotting obediently beside me, and I bought my ticket. Not once, however, but about five times. On each occasion but the last something went wrong: 'The lighting's not right—cut!' or: 'Cut—can you do it again? Somebody else came into shot.' Only Emma seemed unperturbed.

We heard the train approaching. 'Come on, everybody,'

said Robin, 'we've only got a thirty-second stop.' Apparently British Rail had organized a special stop just for our benefit, and had agreed we could hold the train up for precisely thirty seconds. I was amazed. I just could not see how we could all get aboard in that time: cameramen, soundmen, with all their gadgets and lighting equipment, and everyone trailing yards of cable. I wished I'd had a camera myself and could have filmed the pantomime of them all trying to bundle through the same door all at once.

But we made it—well, at least, the train did not go without anyone!

Once on board, everything I did was filmed over and over again. Either the lighting was wrong, or somebody got in the way, or Emma looked in the wrong direction at the wrong moment, or I did the wrong thing.

By the time we had finished with British Rail and were ready for the ironmonger's shop, I was exhausted. But a repetition of the previous minor dramas was to follow. Robin set up everything inside the shop, tried to make sure that nobody else came in while we were making the film and told me what he wanted: 'I want to see you coming up to the door, walking in with Emma, going up to the counter, having a look round, and telling us what you see—including anything you can't identify straight away. Right, off we go. Count ten, and come in.'

Emma and I stood outside the door, I counted ten, and we walked in.

'No, no. That wasn't right.'

'Why? What did I do wrong?'

'We could see you standing there. You'll have to go further back, up the shop window a bit before you approach.'

The shop was in a small block in the middle of a council estate with stretches of grass planted here and there. The ironmonger was situated on the edge of one of these stretches of grass. What I had not realized, going in my normal way along the pavement, was that there was a drop from the shop to the grass on the side. I went outside again, and stood half way along the shop window.

Robin appeared out of the door. 'No, Sheila, further back. Back . . . even more. Further back . . .' So I backed, and Emma backed, and suddenly I disappeared down the drop on to the grass. Needless to say, Emma still had her paws planted firmly on the pavement. She looked over at me as if to say: 'Well, I don't know. You took my harness off, I thought you didn't need me any more. Now look what you're doing—backing off down banks, indeed!' I dusted myself off, and started again.

I was never so glad, at half-past eight that evening, when we had finished the 'wild tracks' in our own living-room, to close the door on the entire crew and have a bit of peace. For all my hard work with Emma, and twelve hours of that day, I think three minutes actually appeared on television. But perhaps, in the context of the programme, it was all worth while. I hope so.

In any case, it was a day's work over and as Don and I sat back that evening I was too tired to consider another work problem which was looming, which had been nagging at me, and which I could not resolve. When I was blind I used to give talks on behalf of Guide-Dogs to all sorts of organizations both in Nottingham and in outlying towns and villages. Weeks before, even before my operation, I had booked a date to give a talk to a Rotary Club. Since I had come out of hospital I had not given a talk and this was the only one arranged, but I had been thinking off and on about it. The point was, the Rotary Club were expecting a blind person with her guide-dog and I had not told them how circumstances had changed. Not only could I see, but I was now not sure whether I could get up and talk to an audience that I could see. It worried me terribly, and now the talk was only forty-eight hours away.

But, for once, tiredness was a blessing. I couldn't think about it there and then, nor discuss it with Don, who would be sure to be helpful. Yet even as I got into bed, I knew the problem would be waiting for me in the morning.

CHAPTER THREE

BREAKFAST-TIME IS not my best time for discussing problems. Some people are fully awake and active from the moment they get out of bed. I belong to the other half of the human race, and take a long time and a lot of coffee before I get into gear. But Don and I managed to make some sense, even at that early hour, of the threatening business of the approaching Rotary Club talk, because I really couldn't put it off any longer and I couldn't solve the problem on my own. My inclination was to pretend that I was still blind and to take Emma on her harness, let her curl up in front of them in her usual way, and for me to give my usual talk, which always went down well and showed people how marvellous guide-dogs are.

But I knew this would be taking the easy way out, and in my heart I knew I couldn't do it because it would be deceitful. Another alternative was to cancel the whole business. I didn't know, in any case, whether I was really up to standing in front of an audience and talking to them. It had been all right when I was blind. I had no idea what the audience looked like and, more important, I didn't know whether they were yawning with boredom or not. Perhaps the reason for my diffidence about the whole thing was that I had come to the end of the road as a speaker on behalf of guide-dogs. Yet, if we cancelled the talk, it would mean a lot of disappointment for the Rotarians, quite apart from it being impossible for them to engage another speaker at such short notice.

In the end, after Don and I had talked it out, we decided that I should ring them, explain the changed circumstances, and see what they said. I tried to get hold of the Chairman all that morning but there was no reply, and there was still no reply that afternoon. I tried another number and managed to get the Secretary's wife, and sat back relieved thinking that's that, secure in the knowledge that he had a message to ring me back. But he didn't ring back. The following day arrived, and by that time it was too late to alter plans, to tell anyone about my being able to see, or to do anything other than be in a state of nerves as I prepared to go off and do the talk. Emma also was not her usual self, perhaps because she saw me get her harness off the hook (even though I intended only to carry it) and was obviously wondering, 'First it's a lead, now it's back to a harness again. What *is* she playing at?'

There was only one consolation. Rotary Clubs had always been my favourite audiences, partly because male audiences always seemed more responsive. This one was a luncheon meeting at an hotel. I got there with Emma, and we sat down in the foyer waiting for the Chairman, or the Secretary who had not rung back. I saw all the men coming in, standing at the bar ordering drinks, and watched some of them glancing in a side-long way at me and Emma with her tell-tale harness, then turning away again. I felt a bit like an exhibit and reflected that this must have been how it always was, but I had not been able to see it.

At last the Secretary arrived—at least I knew it must be the Secretary because of his opening words—but at first that did not interest me as much as the way he approached. He came over and stood in front of me as if I was one of the supporting pillars of the foyer, and sort of talked over me as if I was not really there at all. I wondered if that was what other officials had always done.

'Ah, Mrs Hocken,' he said, 'I'm sorry I couldn't ring you back last night, it was too late . . . but I suppose you were just confirming the booking because we made the date so long ago.'

I looked at him, but his eyes didn't meet mine because he was glancing over his shoulder back to the members at the bar.

'No,' I said, 'that really wasn't it. I had something else to tell you . . .'

But before I could get to the point, he caught my arm and I automatically responded by rising to my feet, then he was propelling me towards the dining-room, saying, 'Well, never mind, we're all looking forward to hearing you.'

'But,' I said, 'there is something—and it's really rather important.'

At last the message sunk in. 'Oh,' he said. 'What is it?'

So I told him.

His expression was a picture: there was no hint of delight and instead a sort of baffled look, with a faint suggestion (or so I thought) of irritation came over his face.

'You can *see*?' he said in a bewildered way, and then in an unconscious pun that I wanted to laugh at, but did not, 'I see!'

'This is what I wanted to tell you about on the phone, because I didn't think it fair that the audience should not know and the point is I think they *should* know.'

He was quite aghast. 'No, no,' he said, 'I don't think that would do.'

'Why not?' I asked.

'Well . . .' he said, obviously not very sure himself, 'I just don't think it would do . . .'

'But I can still tell them all about Emma, and now I can tell the story from two sides, so to speak.'

'Yes,' he said 'I know. But the point is we want to raise money for guide-dogs, and, somehow . . . well, I don't think if you told them you can see it would have the same . . . the same impact.'

'Oh dear,' I said, wishing that the Secretary, the men at the bar and the entire hotel would miraculously disappear and that I was sitting quietly at home minding my own business. We stood there for what seemed ages, with waitresses rushing about and, by now, the members of the Rotary Club coming in and taking their seats, and eyeing in a curious way the scene of their Secretary apparently having an argument with their guest speaker.

I tried once again to convince him. 'It won't really make any difference,' I persisted, 'if I tell them. It really won't take away from how wonderful Emma has been and how guide-dogs are such a boon to blind people.'

'Maybe not,' he said, 'but I still don't think you should tell them.' Then, as an afterthought, he added, 'Or if you do, you ought at least to leave it to the end.'

'Oh, I don't like that,' I said. 'After all, they'll know I can see when I don't walk into things without Emma on harness.'

'No, they won't,' he said. 'Leave it to the end.' And that is what I had to do, because at that moment the Chairman came up. The Secretary introduced us without batting an eyelid and did nothing to suggest that I was other than blind, and the Chairman, a booming, over-jovial character who persisted in calling me 'little lady' which did nothing for my temper, clucked and fussed around me and guided me to my seat at the top table.

'You'll be all right sitting there, little lady,' he said. 'I'm sitting next to you, and I'll announce your talk. All the members are sitting in front of you on tables that branch off this one.'

I sat there, Emma curled up at my feet, nose under the table in her usual impeccable, well-behaved way, and as the soup arrived I stopped being nervous about the talk and became absorbed in the reactions of the men at the other tables. The soup was of the watery kind in which you can see right to the bottom of the plate, and with taste, or no taste, to match. As I started eating I was aware that most of the men, from time to time, were looking at me in a peculiarly furtive sort of way, watching me out of curiosity. It was as if I was about to turn into some prehistoric monster any minute. I put my spoon down, straightened my hair, made sure *that* was all right, and checked that my dress was done up properly in front. Sure enough, it was, and I went back to my soup again. But very uneasily. I looked round and met someone else's gaze, and he looked away. I wondered then if he realized I could see. Or perhaps it had only been a coincidence that I had caught his eye.

Luncheon ended, and the Chairman got up and announced my talk. I got to my feet; Emma, on cue, took a more lively interest in the proceedings; and I was suddenly appalled. I saw what I had never experienced before when getting up to give an address—a mass of faces, some looking intent, some leaning to whisper to the man next to them, some stubbing out cigarettes, some more concerned with what had happened to the wine bottle down the table. It was terrible. I wanted to close my eyes and carry on in the old way, but I knew it was impossible. I had, literally, to face them and to face it. If I was going to continue to give talks I had to accept the sight of my audience, like it or not, and the fact that, give or take cigars, cigarettes, wine or brandy, they were looking at me expecting the goods.

So, somehow, I began. I found it best not to look at the audience at all, but slightly above their heads (which, apparently, most public speakers do anyway although I did not know that at the time). Yet, having solved that problem, another one arose. There were visual distractions that I was not used to. When I had given talks before, my whole mind, my whole being, were concentrated simply on sound—because that is all there was. But now the visual impressions seemed to crowd in on me. I found myself analysing with one bit of my mind the strange, garish, red and gold décor, and wanting to do something about the extravagant Chinese dragons that were breathing fire all over it. I caught sight of a waitress stealthily removing the last of the empty plates. I was fascinated by the hands of a clock which jerked every half minute. And, in an unguarded moment, looking back at the audience, I saw a man glancing at his watch and instinctively I looked at mine. And that put me out of my stride and made me go hot and cold.

But at last came the moment I had been looking forward to least of all, the bombshell for which the entire talk was just a lighted fuse: the revelation that I had had an operation, and could now see.

The result was amazing. Instead of reacting as if they had been taken in by a trick or let down in some way, they burst into applause. The faces that had unnerved me were all, obviously, on my side. Clearly everyone thought the idea was so fantastic, and I was able to continue for another ten minutes, telling them of the utter joy of being able to see, and with Emma now doing her usual tricks. A record amount was raised for guide-dogs that day.

As a result, I decided that I had to go on giving talks. I had been right, I reflected, to have insisted on telling them about my sight. But, to give credit where it is due, the Secretary had also been right in leaving my revelation as, so to speak, a *pièce de résistance*.

Looking back, it was yet one more way in which my life was

43

changed directly as a result of sight. Even after such a short time, there had been startling differences in a way I could never have forecast. I suppose I didn't realize when I was blind what sort of life I was living. I didn't think in a detached way what it was like to be blind, because I had no idea what sight could mean and what a different life sight would give. So many everyday things changed: reading my own mail instead of having it read for me, reading the newspapers, choosing when to take Emma for a walk, going to the shops and being able to look in the windows. Just about everything in life became completely different. It wasn't that I hadn't enjoyed life as a blind person, but when I look back now I feel it was only a part-life. So much is cut off when you are blind, although you don't realize it. Life was a constant struggle. I had Emma, and thank heavens for her, but when we went out it was always a worry that I had to find her harness and put it on and then remember my routes. I had to think about where the tins were in the cupboard. I had to memorize recipes, to remember how much water to add to a packet of soup and how much lard and margarine to put in with flour when baking pies. Life was full of such complications which all vanished with sight. I couldn't just pick up the telephone directory when I wanted to make a call. I had either to ring Directory Enquiries or keep a memory bank of numbers. Admittedly dialling Enquiries was not much trouble, but it had to be done: I just could not do what I wanted to do. There was a part of my life that was not free. I couldn't switch on television and see the pictures, although I could hear it, and so much learning comes from watching television. So many different things were just not available to me.

Sight now seems like a pipeline to me, like oxygen when you are diving in the sea. You can't really live without it, and now I don't understand how people *can* live without it—as I did, and they do.

If things changed for me they also changed for Emma, and nothing more drastically than the application of the 'No Dogs' rule in shops and public places. When I first had Emma, although I had been given the means of mobility and the freedom to go anywhere, I found that having got there very often

Sheila and Don

Sheila and Emma

Sheila, Don, Emma, Betty Greene and Zelda

Betty and Harold Greene

Sheila, Emma, Kerensa, Christmas 1977

Signing sessions

there was still a barrier: NO DOGS. I used to go into shops in those days only to be stopped and turned out of the door. 'No dogs. We don't allow dogs in here.' 'But she's a guide-dog,' I used to say, hoping those magic words would change their minds. 'Oh, it's not me,' they'd reply. It was never them. It was the Ministry of Health or the manager or the local council. 'I'd let you in,' I would be told, 'but if other people see you bringing your dog, everyone will want to bring their dogs in.' And I would be propelled, with Emma, out of the shop.

I discovered that the best way round this situation was to start with the manager or the owner of the premises by either asking to see him when I got there or by ringing up beforehand. I remember wanting to go to our local theatre to see Brian Rix. He was one of my favourite comedians. He could always make me laugh, just by what he said. I rang up. I explained to the girl who answered the telephone that I wanted to see Brian Rix, and I had a guide-dog. 'I'm sorry,' she replied, 'but we don't allow dogs in the theatre.' 'I can understand that,' I replied, 'and I'm sure you don't normally, but she *is* a *guide-dog*, and I can't come without her.' 'I'm sorry. We just don't allow dogs, and I'm afraid that's it.' And that was it, because she put the phone down.

But I desperately wanted to see Brian Rix. When I say 'see', of course, I mean 'listen'. As I have explained, blind people do use the word 'see' partly because to say 'listen' or 'touch' or whatever would only complicate matters, and partly because that would be an admission of not belonging to the normal world. I decided I would have to see the theatre manager. Emma took me up to the box-office, and I tried to sound authoritative when I said, 'Can I see the manager, please?' Finally he appeared, and I heard a voice say, 'I'm the manager, what can I do for you?'

'I want to come and see the Brian Rix show, but you won't let Emma in—she's my guide-dog.' There was a silence for a moment.

'Well, I'm afraid it's our rule that we don't let dogs in normally.'

'I'm sure you don't, but she would be very well behaved. If we could sit in the front row she wouldn't be in anyone's way. And

45

if she *was* any trouble, or made a noise, or if you had any complaints about her during the performance, you could always throw us out. I wouldn't mind, but please give us a try. Emma won't be any bother, honestly.'

I went on telling him about the virtues of Emma, trying to convince him before he made up his mind to say No. But in the end he said Yes. I *was* surprised. 'Well, I'm sure she's well behaved,' he said. 'She looks it. I'll get your ticket for you.'

I was amazed as we walked out of that theatre foyer, and then I realized it was probably not my talking that had done the trick. It was more probably the way Emma had sat there looking at him in a way that would be more pleading than I could ever be. So after that I decided the best way to get in anywhere was to let Emma conduct the interview, to convince any manager by her looks that she was not going to wreck their shops or destroy their theatre. From that moment on I gained a lot more freedom in Nottingham.

But the old problem came back redoubled when I could see. I could no longer use the magic words, 'But she's a guide-dog.' And although I often carry it, she doesn't wear a harness any longer. All of which has made things very difficult from the time of my operation, because I never go anywhere without Emma. I always want her with me, whether it's just a local shopping expedition or a longer journey into the city. I don't think it is fair to leave her behind and, of course, she doesn't understand there are notices forbidding her entry everywhere. I have to try to find shops that don't have a warning sign on them, but they are becoming fewer and fewer because local councils are now encouraging shopkeepers by sending them 'NO DOGS' signs. I am glad to say that now some enlightened shops actually display special signs giving an exception for guide-dogs. Of course, it is up to the shopkeeper whether he puts the signs up or not. There is no law that says he must do it. I can understand, moreover, that there are owners who have no control over their dogs, and they would be a nuisance in shops. In all fairness, there are some places that have let us in regardless of their 'NO DOGS' rule—so I suppose I can say that Emma has been to many places where no dog has ever been before, and she has never chewed the floorboards up. In fact, most of the time people don't realize she is there at all because she is so quiet and curls up in such a small space.

Strangely enough, not long after I had been home from hospital, it was the 'NO DOGS' rule that gave me, yet again, a fresh insight into Emma's character.

One day I had to go to a local shop that used to let Emma in with me when she was a guide-dog but now no longer admitted her. I had already had an argument with the shopkeeper, and didn't want another one. So, for the one and only time in my life, I decided I would leave Emma at home and go on my own. Emma heard me getting the shopping bag and, as usual, rushed to the front door. 'No, Emma,' I said, 'I won't be long. I promise. But I've got to go to this shop, and they won't let you in. I'm ever so sorry, little sausage. Stay there like a good girl.' Emma did as she was told. She stayed there. But 'there' was right at the front door. I tried to lean over her and open it. She would not budge. 'Emma, come on. Let me out.' But she wouldn't move an inch. I took her by the collar and tried to drag her back into the living-room. But no success. She doesn't weigh a great deal, possibly about sixty pounds, yet now she seemed to have put on a ton. She dug her paws into the carpet and refused to move, and she looked up at me with an expression that was fatal. It said: 'You've just *never* been out without me. You can't start doing it now. Whatever it is you want from that shop, you'll just have to go without.' I had to give in.

Don went down for me later when he came back from the surgery, and I took Emma for a walk instead. I was glad that she had persuaded me not to leave her behind, and I was glad I had been forced to keep my resolve not to patronize shops which wouldn't allow dogs, because it was only about a fortnight after this that I had a really extraordinary demonstration which showed that, despite being able to see, I still couldn't do without Emma.

CHAPTER FOUR

WHEN I WAS blind, I used to have a constantly recurring nightmare: it was full of terrifying shapes and threatening sounds, and was, I came to realize, an expression of my utter dependence on Emma and my deep fear of ever being parted from her and having to try to fend for myself. Realization of the meaning did not lessen the desperate terror when it occurred, nor the relief when I woke and found it was not true after all. The pattern was always the same. I was in the middle of Nottingham near Griffin and Spalding's department store, among deafening traffic noise, on the edge of a pavement— with no Emma. Masses of people were jostling and crowding me. I could hear them talking to one another, but when I tried to stop them and ask for help they ignored me and just pushed past when I told them I had lost Emma. At the same time I knew the reason they were all engulfing me like this and taking no notice. It was because they could not see me. Like me, they were all blind.

I used to wake up with the relief of just having escaped death, wildly pleading with Don never to let me go on my own into Nottingham.

Partly as a result of the fear of that nightmare, even though it never recurred after my operation, I sometimes used to take Emma's guide-dog harness with me when we went shopping in the first few months after I could see. My reasons were confused. I had come to rely on the harness as the link with Emma and hence to the outside world. Having Emma on the lead *and* having the harness with me as well seemed an insurance. I knew it was illogical and I knew I should try to break myself of the habit, but there it was.

One afternoon I made a conscious decision to be strong and not to take the harness. I remember my hand hovering near the harness in its place on a hook near the hall-stand, and thinking,

48

No! Emma had seen me make a move into the hall for my coat, and was bouncing about like a vertical take-off dog as she always did when she knew we were about to go shopping, and was wagging her tail so furiously that her entire body was swinging to and fro as well. All this with excited snorts and yelps as I bent down to clip the lead to her collar on which she still kept her little brass disc saying proudly, 'I Am A Guide Dog'. Now that she didn't have to guide me, Emma loved to stop and sniff the trees and the lamp-posts; if we met another dog, well, that was a further treat. Yet, although Emma seemed to have reverted to behaving like other dogs, with the shedding of her responsibilities, there was one important respect in which she did not. It took me some time to realize it, but it gradually dawned on me that she didn't walk on a lead like an ordinary dog: she always walked that bit further in front, always to the left of me (as she did when guiding) and, most noticeably, always kept a slight tension on the lead. This I liked particularly, because, just as she used to communicate with me through the handle of the harness, I felt I was still very much connected with her and we were still an indivisible team when we went out together.

It was like this as we set off on that late February afternoon: Emma pulling gently, like the old days, and enjoying herself so much. We had only gone down to the local shops, but, of course, on the way back there was the obligatory stop at the pet-shop. It was always marvellous to me, now that I could see, to watch how Emma behaved herself—just as she had always behaved herself when a guide-dog and we had gone there, into this canine Aladdin's cave, this very centre of all temptation. Emma sniffed round the shelves and always stopped at one point and looked round and up at me, brown eyes full of question marks, and giving just a tentative wag meaning: 'This looks the sort of thing we're after, don't you think? What about this?' Usually it would be the display of brightly-coloured rubber bones, or sometimes the chewy toys. Occasionally it would be the outsize square biscuits or the tins of vitamin chocolate drops. Whatever it was, Emma would inspect it with enormous interest, but would never touch. I had seen children far worse behaved in sweet-shops than Emma in the pet-shop.

She, unlike the more unruly kids, had been well taught that you can look but not touch.

For some reason, on this particular afternoon she took longer than usual making up her mind what took her fancy, uncharacteristically rather like the kind of woman who has every hat in the shop out on the counter before deciding that what she really wants is a new bra. Emma had looked thoughtfully at blue rubber bones, non-committally at yellow rubber bones, and disdainfully at brown ones. And then given the approving wag of the tail at last to a chewy toy on another shelf that had had a thorough going over. I thought as I paid for it that it looked like one of Don's slippers fashioned in toffee.

With this prize firmly in her mouth we made our way to the door of the shop. While we were in there I had been getting a bit anxious about Emma taking her time over picking and choosing because I knew it was beginning to get dark. My eyesight is fine in daylight but no good at all at night because my retinas—which, over years of blindness, never developed—have insufficient facility for picking out objects in the dark. Having said this, I was only a little apprehensive because much as the dark made me nervous and unsure of myself, we would still be able to get home with the help of the street-lamps. But I was totally unprepared for what did happen when we got out of the shop. Outside the light of the shop window it was not just dark, it was black. At first I thought there was a power cut. I had no idea what to do. Then I found I could just make out the street-lamps. But they were very blurred, just vague blobs of amber. I wear contact lenses, the soft sort, and I wondered if something had gone wrong with them. It reminded me of when I first came out of hospital and wore glasses. I used to forget to clean them and wonder why it was so dark when I got out into the daylight. But the same thing could not happen with contact lenses.

'Gosh, Emma,' I said, 'I know it's dark, but everything's so blurred.' By this time my eyes were beginning to smart, and at last it dawned on me. Fog! The smell should have given it away from the moment we came out of the pet-shop. I had smelt it, but not cottoned on. 'Fog, Emma,' I said almost involuntarily and thinking at the same time that it was almost like being blind again. I was now very worried because it seemed to be getting thicker.

Finally I said, 'It's no use, Emma, we'll have to have a go.' And so, taking her lead firmly, I set off into the blackness. Within a few seconds the light from the window of the pet-shop had vanished behind us, and, to make it worse, the fog had quickly become so thick that even the amber blobs had been swallowed up. All I could see was a sort of soft, swimming haze. I stood wondering what to do. Emma, sensing something was wrong, dropped her chewy toy onto the pavement and I had to fumble to pick it up and put it into my basket. I knew we were still only a few yards from the pet-shop, but I could hardly go back there and ask someone to take us home. There was only one thing for it: if we couldn't go back, we would have to go forward, against the odds. I took a firmer grasp on Emma's lead and pulled her closer to me. 'Emma,' I said, 'I'm sure we're not going to like this.' Emma stepped forward and I followed her. I kept very close to her.

'I don't know how many kerbs we cross,' I said. That was something, when I was blind, that I never failed to note and never forgot. But once I was able to see I had given up the habit of automatically counting kerbs. I had lost the unfailing routine that occurred every time I went out: Turn left on the fifth down kerb, turn right on the fifth up kerb. I had stopped remembering what pavements were like and measuring out a journey by their roughness or smoothness, and whether I felt tarmac, or slabs, or gravel through my shoes. I had also forgotten to remember the echoes that came back from different brick walls and gave sure reference points, punctuated by the differing sound of wooden gates or, quite unmistakable, the hollow ring of a railway arch. I blamed myself as we stumbled along in the fog, quite unnecessarily I suppose. Why hadn't I kept up my old routine? I thought. Why, just because I could see, had I thrown away habits that might always be useful? Yet I knew that the very abandoning of old habits had been part of my celebration of seeing, of joining the rest of the world.

I racked my brains, desperately attempting to remember how many kerbs we had to go up and down. All I could recall, instead, was that there were shops and, after the pet-shop, a big

51

chestnut tree and then a beech hedge that looked so beautiful. All my impressions had become visual, and it didn't help at all. So I walked very gingerly behind Emma.

Emma stopped, and I stopped. I assumed she was sniffing a tree or an interesting piece of grass. 'Come on, Emma,' I said. She didn't move. It was strange, because although I assumed she had stopped to sniff I couldn't feel her through the lead putting her head down, nor could I hear her usual snuffles and snorts. I put my hand down to feel her head. Emma had sat down. I put my foot forward a little into the blackness, and I felt as if I was on a cliff-top or the edge of the world. It was a kerb. Emma had sat down by a kerb, just as she always did when she was a guide-dog. It was, moreover, something she had not done from the moment she knew I could see. Was it just coincidence?

'There's a good girl, Emma,' I said. 'Come on, I know there's a kerb there.' She got up and crossed the road. I was very careful as we neared the other side, trying to find the opposite kerb. I felt Emma hesitate. Yes, there it was. She'd got it. Up we went, and walked on.

The pavement then became very uneven beneath my feet, and all the confidence that had been coming back drained away again because I couldn't remember rough pavement at any stage of our walk. Emma slowed down. 'There's a good girl, Emma. Are we finding the way home?' Then, suddenly, she turned left and I remembered that there was a left turning on our route. This must be it. Then I felt a small grass bank under my feet and recalled all at once that that was right. 'Good girl, Emma,' I said, 'find the way home.' By this time the fog was really dense. It was eerie and disturbing. I could see nothing whatsoever, and I felt I had become involved in one of those time-shift stories and had been transported back to a part of my life, the great dark void, that I never wanted to revisit.

Emma stopped again. Another kerb. And a deep one this time. Thank goodness for Emma. Had I been on my own, I would have fallen down. 'Good girl, Emma.' But before I could put my foot down into the gutter, Emma was backing off on the lead. 'Emma, come on. What's the matter? Come on, there's a good girl.' I thought: Perhaps she really has found a tree with interesting scents this time. I stood still. Then in a few seconds I heard a sound. A hiss of tyres on the road. It was a bike. Emma had heard it long before me, and had, no doubt, seen its lamp.

Only when it was past and there was silence again, the enfolding, strange silence of fog, did she move. Up the next kerb, then a left turn, and almost immediately a sound under my feet that was unbelievable music: the crunch of gravel! We were home!

At the door I put the light on, and saw Emma for the first time since we had left the pet-shop. She was wagging her tail furiously, leaping about as if she was three again and snorting and sneezing with pleasure. She was thrilled because she knew what she had done. I took the chewy toy from my basket and made an enormous fuss of her.

'Emma,' I said, 'how did you know? How did you know? Who is the cleverest girl in the world?' And as she proudly carried the chewy toy slipper, head high, still wagging her tail like a metronome gone mad as she disappeared up the hall, I could tell that she was thinking: 'Yes, but it's not just that I'm clever. I know now that she *still* can't do without me to look after her.'

Not long after this, two events took place that altered the course of my life. The phone rang on a bright day in April, and I little knew then what it would lead to. It was Margaret Howard of the BBC. They had heard of my operation and wanted me to do a programme for them. I was astonished. Although I was always conscious of how wonderful it was to be able to see, I was surprised at the interest other people showed in me as a result. Partly because of this, I think, I did not react with instant enthusiasm to the idea of doing a broadcast. I could not, somehow, immediately see why people should be interested in *me*. Also at the back of my mind I knew straight away that it would mean going to London, and the idea of an enormous city quite scared me. But by the end of the conversation I had accepted and felt very flattered. I replaced the phone, lit a cigarette, sat down and, rather in a daze, said to Emma who was stretched out by the fire: 'Well, Emma, what do you think about that? We're going to London.'

London! The more I thought about it, the more I didn't like

53

it. But if I showed more apprehension than excitement, Don made up for it when I told him. 'Marvellous,' he kept saying, 'what an opportunity.'

By the time the day arrived for Emma and me to catch the London train from Nottingham, he had practically convinced me of how marvellous it all was. And London, though it did not rid me of my dislike of big cities, was not as formidable and scary as I thought it would be. Margaret Howard met me at St Pancras, but it was Emma who really helped to calm my nerves. She got into the waiting taxi as if she had been doing it every day of her life, and, curling up on the floor, proceeded to take no further interest in our journey to Portland Place. Emma, I thought, you've got the right idea. That's the way to deal with London! Nor was she any more impressed by the BBC, where, to my surprise, we had to fight out our customary 'No Dogs' tussle with the commissionaire. In the studio, once again Emma took it all in her stride, and after a preliminary sniff of inspection round the sound-proofing settled down by my feet as I sat at the microphone for the interview.

It all went very well, and afterwards one of the producers, who was pleased with the result, said to me: 'You ought to write a book about it all.' And I smiled, took it as a graceful compliment and thought no more about it.

But fate has a way of providing coincidences to emphasize the way life is meant to go. A few days later I was turning out a cupboard and came across a folder full of braille transcriptions on foolscap-size brown card. At first I couldn't think what they were. I ran my fingers over a page and then it all came back: my poetry, written years ago when I was blind. I sat down and re-read the poems, and it struck me how sad they all were. Some were about myself and blindness, and many were about animals. Here is one I had written back in 1969:

The Tunnel

I stumble and there I lie resting and in
My tunnel of darkness I cry.
Only the black damp walls
Echo back in reply.

54

Despair and hope are feelings
Long since gone.
The fear of dying in my loneliness
Is driving me on.
With jagged rocks and sharp stones
My path is lined
Tearing at my soul and
Piercing my mind.
The only way is forward
My tunnel has no retreat
No words of encouragement
Only threat of defeat.
It's hard to remember my reasons
For coming to such a place.
Was it to hide?
No, not to hide
My face.

No, I did not choose this fate
And yet I came this way
Surely not in search
Of such misery and decay.
If death lies in my path
There'll be no fear nor regret
But life is too cruel a thing
To relinquish her debt.
No life or death is here
Just a never-ending void.
No sleep, no peace until
My very being is destroyed.

I put the poetry aside. How did I write it? It was as if someone
else, certainly not the present me, had written the poems. I
could not write poetry now. I realized what a different person
I had become with sight. I had not written a line of poetry
since being able to see, and the folder that I had just closed
contained mostly, it seemed, a rather sad insight into the
person I once was. Not that I actually felt sad or self-pitying
at the time, but the poetry proved that inside I must have

been miserable without recognizing what it was like to be miserable.

Never having had real sight, I wasn't like the person who has been fully sighted and then goes blind, so therefore understands the outside world and also understands what they are missing. I thought I was quite happy as a blind person, and I did all the things that I felt I wanted to do—or, putting it another way, I didn't think that my blindness stopped me from doing anything. Yet I was not free. I was not free from people wanting to help me, or that constant, 'Oh, she's blind so she can't do this,' or people apologizing for saying, 'Did you see so and so?' They would often ask me if I had seen a programme on television, then: 'Oh, I'm sorry. I forgot. How awful of me.' And that was more embarrassing than ever.

Now that process has been reversed, and when I first got my sight back people would say, 'Did you hear the television last night?' or, 'Feel this.' And follow up with, 'Oh, of course, you can see now. I'm sorry.' They apologized to me until they got used to the idea that I could see. And, of course, people treat you differently when you can see. They treat you, at last, as an equal. However well people used to know me when I was blind there was never that equality, and if I asked them to do something for me—even if it was quite unrelated to my blindness— I always felt that I was inferior and that the sighted person could, in superiority, wave the magic wand and give me what I wanted. So I was beholden to the sighted world for the things I needed, and now it's so lovely because whenever I ask someone to so something for me it's just that in itself, and I am equal.

I put the folder of poetry back in the cupboard wondering if all poets were sad by nature. Byron and Browning were two of my favourites and I realized that they showed anguish and longing in their poetry. But they also wrote about happier moments as well. At the same time my mind went back to the producer's remark at the BBC, and I thought: If I no longer feel capable of writing sad poetry, why shouldn't I write a happy book?

That was the first thought I had of writing what eventually became *Emma and I*. And the more I thought about it, the more tempting and exciting the idea became. I remembered all the evening classes I had been to when I was blind learning about writing, and I became more and more confident. By the time Don came in from the surgery, I was bursting to tell him. 'Fantastic,' he said, and listened to all my ideas. Yet all the time we were talking I had the notion that his mind was not entirely on my great project.

It transpired that while I had something to tell him, he also had some news for me, but I had got in first. At last he explained.

'Harold rang this afternoon,' he said. (Harold was his cousin who lived up in Yorkshire.) 'They're thinking of going to Skye for their holidays and they wondered whether we would like to go with them—round about the end of the month, after Easter. What do you think?'

I didn't really know what to think. The idea of writing a book had, in only an hour or two, become such a huge balloon of fantasy that a holiday in Skye seemed a strange, alien signal beaming in from another planet.

'Well,' I said, as the idea began to sink in, 'it sounds terrific, but I don't know much about Skye. Could we get some brochures?' Then I added, having suddenly remembered that Harold and his wife Betty had a Weimerana dog called Zelda, 'I suppose they're bound to be taking Zelda with them. And Emma could play with her. That would be nice.'

In fact, although I didn't want to disappoint Don, I was not as thrilled as I might have been at the idea of a holiday. Apart from being keen to start the book, I also had misgivings about holidays in general. I remember how, when I couldn't see, we had set off for holidays with the highest hopes but they had never failed to turn out, in all honesty, a total waste of money and time.

Once we went to Cornwall. Don had picked a very picturesque old inn by the River Fowey, with a balcony so that he could watch the big ships, the yachts and the little boats going up and down to the sea. But I would just sit there and be so bored, and not know how to occupy myself. It used to make me feel so sad, because we would go for a walk and Don would say, 'The scenery's beautiful here. The sea looks really blue, and it's lapping against the cliffs and up the sand, and there are so many wild flowers.' But for all Don's lovingly-meant descriptions, I

57

could not visualize what Cornwall was really like. It could have been the moon. So holidays were a bit of a sad time and I was always glad to get home, because I knew my home and it didn't matter there that I couldn't see.

However, in due course, Harold sent the brochures on Skye. They looked wonderful and we decided we would go. I persuaded myself that in the mountain air I might get even more inspiration for the book; but I also knew it would be yet another test of my experience with sight, and, although life had taught me never to look forward too much, I just hoped that this might turn out to be the first holiday I had had without disappointment.

CHAPTER FIVE

DESPITE MY MISGIVINGS, I was excited about the holiday. And it would be a holiday for Emma too—Emma's first *real* holiday, when she would have absolutely nothing to do except romp, nobody to worry about, and, what is more, another dog to play with.

We had arranged to meet Harold and Betty with Zelda at the end of the motorway north of Stirling. It was a sparkling spring day as we set off, and as we came up into Scotland I was fascinated by the way the land started to rise, not really in mountains, but fells as they call them. And as we reached Callander it was *me* this time saying to Don, 'Look! Just look at that. Isn't it fabulous! Look at that mountain.' I didn't realize then that it was not truly a mountain in that part of Scotland, but to me it looked like it: beautiful golden green, stretching up into the sky. In Callander, the *Dr Finlay's Casebook* town, I saw the incredibly tiny streets and houses with windows that were bowed and had lots of different little panes—it was like a dream, but one I could never have dreamt because I had no inkling of its existence before that moment.

As soon as we got to our hotel I made sure all the luggage had been taken inside, and then we went out to explore. I couldn't wait. Luckily Don was also just as keen to see the sights because he had never been to Scotland before either. So we left Harold and Betty to unpack while we went off into the streets and the little narrow alleys of Callander. Emma was as excited as we were. She always loved different places, different surroundings, and she didn't care where she was as long as we were all together. But Callander was something else again, something altogether different from anything she had previously experienced. Grass was growing out of the sides of the pavements. There were lots of dogs about, and even the lamp-posts were different and somehow very Scottish-looking. With the dogs she could stop and discuss the time of day, or simply bark at them and it didn't matter. Her harness was hundreds of miles away in a south-easterly direction. We let her off the lead as we climbed up the hillside behind the town to look at the little cottages. It was so wonderful to be able to watch Emma rummaging in and out of the hedgerows, popping into the little garden gates and back out again, and being thoroughly and hurriedly busy, quartering here and there with her nose down, and suddenly stopping from time to time at a specially interesting and new Scots smell.

The houses nestled at the sides of the roads that climbed up steeply into the sky. They were not like any houses that I had ever seen before—they were tiny cottages, all cleanly painted in white or sometimes pink. How different from the red brick terraces of Nottingham which was how I imagined all houses were!

The next day we set off from Callander on the last lap north-wards, to take the ferry over to Skye. On the way we started to climb into the really mountainous area: suddenly they were there, above us as we started to climb a snake-like bend. To someone who had not seen anything like it before it was wonderful, but to Don it was marvellous as well. It took our breath away as we saw all the mountains, reaching up, stretching away to the distance, all snow capped. The sun was out and it glistened and seemed to stream down the mountain nearest us, like icing streaming down a cake. Then it was gone, hidden behind a mountain on the other side, and I could see the grass again which was golden rather than green. And down lots of the mountains ran streams, falling and dancing down the mountainside like cascades of diamonds.

'Don,' I said, 'it's so beautiful. I never thought anywhere so beautiful was so near to home, in the same land I live in.'

We climbed up little roads and looked down, right down below us, into lochs that mirrored the mountains in them, and the grasses round their sides, and the sun and blue sky. Nearer to Mallaig the roads were even narrower with only enough room for one car, and trees hung right over so that for much of the time we were so shaded it was almost like night. It was like entering into a fairyland where no one lived, but people were just allowed to come and look.

At Mallaig we drove on to the ferry, and I watched the sea-gulls come and alight on the guard-rails round the boat. That was marvellous. I had never seen them so close; I could have touched them. I wanted to hear that song *Over the Sea to Skye* so strongly that it took me over, and Don and I stood there and sang—and it was like a honeymoon really to us, again.

As the Scottish mainland got smaller and smaller, I saw that Emma had become very alert. She was watching the seagulls very intently. People on the ferry were feeding them scraps. 'Oh, Emma,' I said, 'you wouldn't want to steal dinner off those poor seagulls, would you?' She looked up at me, indicating quite clearly, 'Yes, I would,' and with a lust in her eyes as if food had been invented in that very moment. 'Oh, Emma, how wicked of you!'

When we reached Skye, I saw that the green had gone and had been totally replaced by the golden-brown colour of what I supposed was bracken or gorse. There was green on the trees, but a completely different green from anything I had ever seen. Even the flowers seemed to be different colours. After a drive over more mountain roads we reached the inn where we were staying. It was an old shooting lodge at the foot of a mountain and in front of a loch surrounded by rhododendron bushes, which gave it, to me at least, an appearance of deep mystery.

One of the things that struck me as soon as we landed on Skye was the presence of so many sheep. I had never really seen sheep before. I had been aware of them at a distance, in fields, but had been conscious only that they were part of the land-scape, never that they were individual beings. Now here they were, right in front of me as I sat in the car.

'Don, look at those sheep!'

'Yes, aren't they tame? They don't move out of the way at all.'

'Well, they'll get run over.'

Even Emma was taking an interest and sat up on the back seat, peering curiously out of the window and obviously wondering: 'Strange! What strange creatures. Whatever are they?'

As we got nearer to the sheep they moved out of the way as Don pipped his horn and slowed down to let them move to the verges. We were lucky to be there in spring, for there were a lot of lambs as well. Even if there had been no other scenery on Skye I think I should have been quite happy spending my week just watching the sheep.

I am glad to say that Emma, once out of the car, took no further notice of the sheep. I wish I could say the same for Zelda. She was immediately possessed with the idea of chasing them, so our first walk with Harold and Betty was not the quiet peaceful outing we had expected. Zelda careered off into the distance after some sheep and Harold, to my utter astonishment, underwent a total character-change before my very eyes.

I must explain that Harold is in his middle-age, has a very soft, gentle voice and, coming from Brough just outside Hull, has a pleasant Yorkshire accent. In addition he is always so calm and pleasant—at least that is how I had always seen him up to that moment. His wife, Betty, also has a very gentle way with her, and whenever we have visited them they have always been, like all the Yorkshire people I have ever known, most hospitable and welcoming.

So these quiet, comfortable people were with us on this mountainside in Skye. Harold always carries a walking stick with him and at the point where Zelda took off like a dog possessed after the sheep, Harold threw this stick into the air, waved it madly and generally went berserk, shouting, 'Come back, Zelda! Come back here, you stupid bitch!'

I was astounded. I looked at him, and his face was going redder and redder. 'Harold,' I said, 'that won't do any good. She'll come back in her own time.'

But he wasn't listening to me. 'Wait till she comes back. I'll teach her.' And he waved the stick even more furiously.

And Betty, standing beside him, was just as angry. 'Zelda, Zelda, you wicked dog!' She was shouting.

In the end, Zelda did come back—not a bit ashamed—and things calmed down, but I couldn't get over the sight of these two normally calm, friendly people doing a sort of war dance, with Harold throwing his stick and behaving like a wild man. In turn, Harold took an instant and irrational dislike to sheep, partly, I suppose, because he felt so upset that his dog had chased them and partly because he felt that the sheep should not be allowed to roam. It was as well that there were no farmers on hand to witness this little scene because I feel they would have been even more angry than Harold and Betty.

I, on the other hand, was fascinated by the sheep. I longed to touch them, but, tame as they were, they ran off every time we got close to them. Then suddenly, I realized something. I said to Don, 'Have you noticed that they've all got black feet, and ears, and faces, and tails? And sort of beige-coloured bodies?'

'Yes,' he said, 'they're Highland sheep.'

'Yes, I know. But every time I look at one it reminds me of a huge, woolly Siamese cat.'

'Oh Sheila,' he said, 'how can you say that?'

'No—look at the coat patterning. They *are* like Siamese.'

He looked again and finally agreed. 'Yes,' he said. 'You're right, they're black in all the same places that Ming is.'

'I wonder if it's for the same sort of reason, a mutation?'

'I don't know,' said Don. 'You're the expert on that. You'd better ask one of the sheep-breeders—practically everyone round here seems to breed sheep. Why don't you ask the barman at the hotel? He's got some, I know.'

In Siamese cats a mutation gene has restricted the coat colour pattern. The theory is too complicated to explain quickly, but whenever you breed Siamese to Siamese they all get the same coat pattern. I wondered if the same thing occurred with the Highland sheep. When we were having a drink that evening at the hotel, I said to the barman: 'Can you tell me something about the sheep?'

'Aye,' he said in that sing-song Skye accent, 'I breed them.'

'Well, it's strange. They remind me of the Siamese cats I breed. Do your sheep have a mutation gene that restricts the coat colour?'

He looked at me long and hard, took a thoughtful swig oₓ the malt whisky that was never far from his hand, and said nothing.

'They've all got black faces, and black feet, and black tails,' I said. 'What's the reason?'

There was a further silence. Finally the barman said, 'Aye . . . aye . . . they always come like that.'

And that was as far as I got in my research into sheep-breeding.

One morning, for a bit of a lark really, Betty and I decided to go horse-riding. I had not ridden since the day (and, looking back, I must have been mad) when, unable to see a thing, a girlfriend had taken me riding in Sherwood Forest. I had ridden a hard-mouthed brute called Rocky who had proved to be well-named. He had taken off with me at a thousand miles an hour and scared the wits out of me. Yet my chief concern, I remember, had been that the stables would not realize I was blind!

Now I was in charge, and wondered how it would turn out. Betty had never ridden in her life before. Don and Harold said they would come with us and bring the dogs, but decided against actually riding. We booked at Macdonald's Riding School and set off. We found it down a dirt track on a mountainside, and also discovered that the reality was not as grand as the title.

A sort of decrepit shed stood there, and *how* it stood there I do not know. Perhaps it was sheltered in the lee of the mountainside, but it seemed that the lightest Scottish breeze would have blown it over. It looked as if it dated from the very first discovery of Skye. As we were staring at it from the car a little old man emerged, wizened, brown and wrinkled in the face. But you couldn't really see a lot of him. He wore an old jumper, and when I say 'old' I mean it was matted with age and seemed to cling to him as if it had actually grown on him. You couldn't see anything of his neck because the jumper reared up round his chin and his ears. It was met by an old tweed cap with a peak on it that was tied on with a piece of string, and the cap had obviously seen better days as well. Tiny, shrewd eyes peered out from hooded eyelids.

'I hope he's not running the place,' I said to Don. 'He doesn't look as if he could put a bridle on, let alone give riding lessons.'

'No,' said Don, 'he won't own it. Come on, don't worry.'

We got out of the car, and Emma went up and sniffed curiously, first the air around him, then his boots, then his ankles and then his legs. I think she could hardly believe her

64

ose that so many scents of such antiquity could exist in one place.

'How d'ye do,' he said, 'My name is Alasdair Macdonald.'

Oh, I thought, Macdonald. He obviously *does* own the place.

We all shook hands.

'You'll be the Hockens,' he said. 'Aye, well I've not got ye booked for four, only two.'

We explained. 'Aye, well . . . I've not been feeling too well ately. So will ye be goin' out on your own?'

I told him that Betty couldn't ride at all.

'Aye, well did you no say *you* could ride?'

'Er, well yes, I did.' I didn't want to go into the entire business of saying that when I had ridden I couldn't see. In fact, I had no idea what to expect and was really relying on someone competent coming out with us.

I could hear Don making noises of suppressed laughter behind me. I turned and gave him a look. How could he laugh at this poor, frail old man? Then, when I turned back, I saw Alasdair Macdonald was holding a bottle of golden-coloured liquid in his hand. He touched me on the arm confidentially and said, 'Will ye no be having a wee dram with me?'

It was ten o'clock in the morning. I thanked him but said that I would not be having a wee dram. Carried on the breeze came a powerful hint of a uniquely Scottish kind of medicine for any ailment that Alasdair Macdonald might be suffering from.

'Aye, well. I might be able to get into the saddle. But I have to have a bit of me medicine before I go out on the fells.'

Harold and Don stood there, and Betty and I knew they were waiting to see what a hash we made of mounting our ponies when they eventually arrived.

'Will ye join me in a wee dram?' Alasdair Macdonald said to Don and Harold.

'Ah . . . no thanks, old lad,' said Harold. 'It's a bit early for me. But don't let us stop you.'

'I can see ye're understandin' folk. Will you come into the shed a minute?'

He led the way into the tumbledown shed. It had stirrups hanging on bits of string and saddles strewn about the floor. But there was hardly space for them on account of the stacks of old whisky and brandy bottles in every corner. Once inside, Alasdair Macdonald flourished the bottle again.

'I think I could do with some of that,' said Betty. 'I've never been on a horse before. You'd better let me have a nice tame one.'

'Och . . . they're all nice little tame ones. I train them all mysel'. '

I didn't much like the sound of that. I could not, stretch my imagination as I might, visualize him breaking in a horse. I had immediate visions of Betty and me galloping in all directions up the mountainsides, with Harold and Don laughing, and Emma and Zelda looking on in bewilderment.

'Do you live here?' asked Don, as another dose of medicine was being self-administered.

'Aye. Born and bred here. Lived here all my life. I've never wanted to go anywhere else.'

'Have you never been to the mainland?' I asked him.

'Aye, I did just the once, you know.'

'Oh, did you? Did you come down to England?'

'No, I went down to Edinburgh. But it was a bit too rushed for me. Too much traffic. I would no want to live in a place like that. Give me Skye, it's nice and peaceful.'

'When did you go?' Don asked.

'Ah, let's see . . . it would be nineteen forty-seven.'

'Nineteen forty-seven!' I said in disbelief. 'My goodness. You haven't seen what it's like now? Have you seen . . . er . . . traffic lights?'

He looked at me with a blank expression.

'. . . and what about zebra crossings . . . traffic jams . . . sky-scrapers . . .?' I went on a wild catalogue of the doubtful benefits of civilization.

He shook his head. 'No, I don't think I have. No.'

It was odd, I thought, that in only a few months of sight I had probably seen more than Alasdair Macdonald had in his entire life. When he spoke, too, it was as if he inhabited his own self-contained world. His voice was quiet, and in the middle of a sentence you thought he might fall asleep and not finish it. Then, when you were thinking of saying something else to prevent the conversation from ending, he would continue.

There was another empty 'medicine' bottle to add to the pile before we stepped outside again. Understandably perhaps, Alasdair took quite a time to round up and saddle and bridle three ponies, and then he took about five tries before he finally succeeded in getting on to his pony, and it was not very tall. Betty wanted to show her keenness and the fact that, although she was a beginner, she was not daunted. I could see by her face that she thought the small pony he had given her was the size of a hunter, but she was not going to give in. She got on the mounting block, took an enormous leap, missed the pony completely and landed over the other side. We tried not to laugh, and Harold almost had heart failure.

Eventually we were all mounted, and off we went up the side of the mountain. Sitting there on the pony, even though it was not very big, I began to think I was a long way from the ground and that I preferred, in this instance, not being able to see. We were only walking, so I was able to keep calm for the time being. But then we started going down the side of the mountain, a very steep side, and that horrified me—to see from the top of the pony this distant vista below that moved wildly with every step. I felt quite out of control. Although they were mountain ponies and were very sure-footed I felt anything but safe, and when we got to a piece of slippery ground and my pony did not handle it very well I had to hold on to the saddle until he managed to stop himself slipping and canter on. Betty was in an even worse plight. Her pony slipped on the same piece of ground. I heard her shouting frenziedly at me, but I couldn't do anything.

Alasdair would save her, I thought. I looked round. Alasdair was nowhere to be seen.

'Betty!' I shouted. 'Hold on to the reins. Hang on to your saddle!'

'Aaagh!' she screamed. 'Help!'

I turned back to try and help her, but luckily she managed to keep her seat and the pony began to follow mine back up the mountain.

'Where's Alasdair?' I said when we had rejoined one another.

'I don't know,' she said breathlessly. 'I looked round when my pony started to slip, but he'd disappeared. What do you think's happened?'

'What do you mean, "What do you think's happened?" He should be worried about us, not us about him.'

'I know. But did you see how much whisky he'd put away? I don't think we're safe. I think we ought to make our way back.'

It was the best idea, but unfortunately I had no idea how to get back. I was still no good at remembering visual routes. I had always remembered the way by hearing and smell and other senses, and I had certainly taken nothing in of that kind on the way. Luckily the ponies remembered where home was, and headed back in the right direction. I tried to get mine to trot but he refused. After his little flourish down the mountain he obviously considered that was enough excitement for one day, and he would walk back.

We arrived at the shed feeling sure that Alasdair would be there, no doubt having more medicine. But he had not got back. Don and Harold came out to meet us.

'That was quick, lass,' said Harold. 'Are you all right?'

'I'm fine,' said Betty, 'but we've lost Alasdair.'

'You've *what*?'

'We've lost Alasdair Macdonald.'

'How can you have lost him? He went out with you.'

'Yes. But we went over a mountain and when we looked round he'd disappeared.'

We dismounted and stood there wondering what to do. About twenty minutes went by and then, in the distance along the dirt track, we saw Alasdair's pony. He was walking beside it.

'Aye,' he said as he reached us. 'I'm afraid I had a wee accident. I'm sorry if ye missed me. It was ma pony. I could nae control him, and ma leg was playing me up. So I thought I'd better walk.'

We were glad we didn't know this sort of thing was going to happen before we went out, but Alasdair said no more about it. He took us again into his shed, where he kept us for about an hour with endless stories about Skye.

'Ye see that field over yonder?' he crooned, indicating with a brown sinewy hand. Behind his little cottage, which looked as if it had one bedroom and one other room, was a field which might have been fenced at one time.

'Aye. 'Twas in that field my mare foaled,' he said quietly. Alasdair often repeated himself as if he were addressing backward six-year-olds. 'Foaled . . . foaled she did, in that very field.' He looked at us to make sure we were all paying attention. We were. We were fascinated.

'It was one summer night, and I heard a sound, and I crept to the window, and there I saw my mare. Thirty-four she was, thirrrty-four—well, I was a *wee* bit concerned, because, do you know . . . I saw this small wee thing next to her. Next to her it was, right in the field. I could see its coat in the moonlight. Aye . . . well I thought I'd better go out and have a look so I put my clothes on and . . . you'll never guess . . .' He looked at us, his eyes intent and shining at the memory.

'No,' we all said, because we knew he expected it, 'what was it?'

'Why . . . she'd had a foal. A foal at thirrrty-four!'

We all said how wonderful it was, and then managed to make our excuses and get away—but only on condition that we came back and saw him again.

As we were leaving, he took Don by the arm and beckoned him aside.

'You must mind one thing, though,' he said.

'What's that?' said Don.

'You must mind the tale of the folk who come to Skye on holiday.'

Don didn't know what to make of this. Alasdair looked round rather in a conspiratorial way as if he was afraid that something beyond the mountains might overhear him.

'Aye, well . . . it's a fruitful place, is Skye.' He looked round again and his voice dropped to a whisper. 'There may be a wee thing about Christmas time.' He patted Don on the arm, and in the same instant was gone.

And of the magical things about that holiday in Skye, the holiday I had been so unsure about, the prophecy of Alasdair Macdonald proved to be the most magical thing of all.

CHAPTER SIX

WE WERE SAD when the time came to drive back on to the ferry and Skye began to diminish towards the horizon. All my misgivings about going on holiday and whether it would be a success had long since evaporated. I watched the Cuillins sinking into the sea in the far distance. I had been fascinated by the Cuillins, the great, high mountains of Skye. To me they seemed like people. Perhaps it was because I had not been able to see for very long, but I tended—and for that matter, still do— to attach personalities to things. Trees are different personalities to me because they are all shaped so differently, and I found that the Cuillins were like this. They gave me a feeling of knowing them in a strange way. I used to look at them, black and awesome, seeming to exert a power over the entire island, and somehow they also seemed to have power over the people of Skye, making them what they were, preventing them from moving with the times as people had on the mainland for better or worse, and ensuring that Skye went on as it had done for thousands of years. Perhaps it was just a fancy, but that is how the mountains made me feel.

No doubt I had caught, as the song says, 'the tangle of the isles'. One day we had been on a trip from Skye, north across the Minches, over the water to Harris in the Outer Hebrides. On the ferry across, Harold and I, Zelda and Emma, stood on the upper deck at the guard-rails. Harold is such a warm-hearted person that I felt he was as thrilled to be sharing what I was seeing as Don always was. Don had gone below with Betty because it was so windy. Emma and Zelda stood there sniffing the sea wind, and the expressions on their faces translated all the fascinating scents that came off the shore. It was so marvellous to watch Emma and see her reactions. I had so often felt vibrations on the harness and had to guess at what she was seeing. Now I could watch her. Harold looked down at

Emma, seeming to know what I was thinking. He gave her a pat.

'Good girl, Emma. You're a good girl.' And he turned to me, adding, 'She knows you can see, all right.'

'Yes,' I said, 'she does.'

'She's not daft, that dog,' he said.

That, I thought, she certainly is not, and my mind went back to the day that Emma had first realized I could see: when stealthily she was about to steal some of the cats' food, and I said, 'Yes, I can see you, Emma!' Poor Emma, she spun round, amazed and shocked at the same time and life was never quite the same again.

I watched the waves beating against the bows of the ferry, turning white as they were parted, and tossing up in a lovely spray. And the clouds were fascinating. It was really windy and they were sweeping past us in the sky. It was so exhilarating.

When we reached Harris the first thing I noticed was its barrenness. The grass was not really grass at all, just edges of brown that grew out of the sides of the roads. It was not at all like Skye.

'I don't think I'd like to live here,' I said to Don. 'There's a strange feeling that we're right on the very edge of the world.' But this was only a first impression.

'And there don't seem to be any sheep,' Don said with a smile.

'Did you hear that, Harold?' I said. 'No sheep!'

'Well, thank goodness for that anyway,' he said. 'You can have a good run, Zelda old girl.' So we set off for a walk with the two dogs happily romping ahead of us. As we rounded a bend in the road I saw the most beautiful beach beneath us, with a sea that was turquoise blue, a genuine turquoise, more vivid than any on a holiday postcard. The sand was a silvery colour, a dazzling silver. Don and Emma and I were first down to that beach. I ran along and looked back every so often to see my footmarks in the sand. Everyone else laughed at me. But I felt like a child again, and really wanted to stop and build sandcastles!

I watched Emma. Her tail was in the air, wagging, her nose was in the sand and she left a furrow as she shuffled it all up in front of her. It was the most beautiful beach I had ever seen. Don and I looked and looked along its length. It was not only beautiful, but lonely in the friendliest way. We felt as if nobody had ever been there before and we were the discoverers. It was the sort of place I had dreamt of, the ideal of beauty and peace, with the sea just sighing in the background. Even when I was blind I knew that somewhere such a place existed, and now we had found it.

I was thinking of this beach as the ferry took us back to the mainland, and again on the drive back to Nottingham. When we reached Nottingham, and life gradually returned to normal, the memories of Skye and particularly of this beach became a sort of mirage in the mind and I sometimes wondered, as I went about the house, whether we had experienced it at all.

But I was reminded of Skye quite forcibly a few weeks later. I had decided I ought to go and see my doctor. He examined me and said, 'Well, Mrs Hocken, with any luck it should be about Christmas time.' Apart from confirming what I already suspected, I couldn't help smiling. The doctor thought it only too natural that I should appear delighted. He didn't know that apart from that I was, in reality, recalling Alasdair Macdonald's prophecy: 'There may be a wee thing about Christmas time.'

This was in the spring of 1976, and we were still living in the little council pre-fab which Emma and I had moved to before I had met Don and we had married. His own house, with his surgery built at the back and separate from the house, was still occupied by his first wife and would be until she could find some other suitable accommodation. Of course, it takes time to find the right property and to sort things out, but we had arranged that when she did so we would move into the house. In the meantime we were in our little prefabricated bungalow: nice enough for Don, Emma and me, but when I found I was pregnant, it made me impatient to move. I became rather moody about the whole business because there simply was not enough room for an addition to the family. I think poor Don had quite a lot to put up with in those days. Every night when he came home I greeted him and said, 'Anything arranged yet on the house?'

'No, not yet. Don't worry.'

72

'Oh, Don, I don't want to have the baby here. It really is too small,' I would say, thinking also that I had really begun to dislike the place.

'Don't worry, petal. We'll have moved long before the baby comes along.'

But the move was not my only worry. I also thought constantly about Emma and how she was going to react. By the time the baby was born, Emma would be twelve. She had never had a baby in the house, and I didn't want to upset her. I didn't want her to feel that she was being pushed out in her old age. I remember making it quite clear to Don: 'Now Emma will always sleep by our bed, won't she, in her basket?'

'What do you mean?' he said.

'Well, I want that to be Emma's special thing. She'll always be there, and the baby will have her own room.'

'Of course,' Don said, 'I think in any case, that babies should be started off in their own room from the word go.'

At least I had that bit of comfort. I just hoped that Emma would forgive me. I hoped desperately she wouldn't turn away from me because she thought I had a new pet, which is how I supposed a baby might appear to her.

After months of worrying, and only a few weeks before the baby was due, we were at last going to move. Don rang up one day to tell me the date had been fixed. That evening he said, 'Have you packed most of the stuff?'

'Well, just about,' I said, because I had been packing for ages. We had been living for months in between tea chests and cardboard boxes.

'Right. I'll get hold of the removal men tomorrow—and we still haven't done anything about carpets and curtains for the new house.'

It was not really a new house, of course, to him. But it was for us. Carpets and curtains would help to make it a new place, and we had to decorate a room for the baby. I knew Emma would like it there because there was a much bigger garden for her and just over the road a path led into open fields where I knew she would have endless pleasure.

When moving day came and we started to shift the furniture and take up the carpets we had rather a shock. The bungalow

73

had always been very damp, and condensation and leakages everywhere had not helped matters either. In the living-room Don had tried to damp-proof by putting extra wallpaper on one of the walls.

'What do you think of that!' he'd said when he finished. He had put a brick-style paper on. 'Looks solid as well. That should keep the damp out.' I remember him standing back to admire it. He had been really proud of his work. He had taken his decorating overalls off—which are not often used, I might add —and sat, just looking at his wallpaper. 'Really does look good, doesn't it? Don't you think it looks good?'

'Yes, it looks very nice.' But then, even as we were admiring it, part of the corner began to curl up and peel off, as if an invisible hand was taking it off the wall. We stared in disbelief, and then it happened at another corner. Don went up to the wall and tried to press it back into place. But it persisted in coming off again and as soon as one piece was pressed back another peeled off. It was like a Laurel and Hardy film.

We tried everything, but nothing would stop the paper from coming off, and at last Don ended up by using drawing pins. We used to tell our friends that it was the latest fashion to put up your wallpaper with drawing pins. When we came to move, the wallpaper took rather a beating. We moved the sideboard, which had been at the opposite end of the living-room wall from the one that Don had tried to insulate with paper. As soon as the sideboard had been moved out of position, we noticed the wall behind it had turned a nasty colour, and suddenly— yes, the wallpaper fell off.

'My word,' said Don, 'it's a good job we're leaving here.'

And in every room, as soon as the furniture was pulled away from the wall and the beds were packed up and gone, the wall-paper gradually started to peel and fall on to the floor. It was a peculiar experience to see the home that I had lived in for years become a shattered, damp shell, with a terrible, fusty smell about it. When your furniture's gone your house really is empty, as if you had never really lived there. You don't love it any more; you only loved it when all your belongings were around you and it looked so cosy and welcoming. When you get to the reality of just walls, windows and doors, it is a totally different place. I had thought I would be sad to move from there in the end, despite my growing dislike of it since I had become pregnant. But I was not at all sad when I took a last look round and saw those bare rooms with wallpaper peeled off and lying forlornly on the floor.

I went into hospital for only a couple of days to have the baby because it had been made clear that I would not be allowed to keep Emma in the hospital and I hated the idea of leaving her behind. I had really wanted to have my baby at home, because I think having a baby at home is the most natural thing in the world. Having watched my cats have babies, I felt I knew all about it. I also felt that to take anyone out of their natural surroundings and put them in a strange place, with strangers around them, was a hard thing to accept. But no one would listen. The rules of the National Health Service decreed that I had to go into hospital.

The expected date for the new arrival was just as Alasdair Macdonald had predicted all those months before. Christmas Eve. Three nights before, I started having contractions. I was totally unprepared. I hadn't packed my case, as it advised in all the leaflets handed out at ante-natal clinics. But then, I didn't set much store by some of the advice. The list of 'do's' and 'don'ts' was incredible. 'Don't move house.' Well, I suppose, there was some sense in that. But underneath it said, 'Don't catch a cold.' That was when I decided I could not guarantee that I would comply.

We hadn't been in the new house long, and we were still not straight. For one thing we were being re-wired and only two lights worked in the entire place, one upstairs and one downstairs. It had a depressing effect on me because I was experiencing unavoidable dark again. It was about half-past ten at night. Don had been very late in the surgery—he normally doesn't finish anyway until after nine—and we were having a meal. Suddenly I put my fork down and said,

'Don, something strange is happening.'

He sort of dropped everything.

'What? What . . .? What's happening?'

'Well, I don't know. But I do know it's odd.'

'Goodness. Where's your case?'

'Er . . . I haven't packed it.'

'Well, come on, you'd better do it now.' He got up and rushed round in circles. It was strange, but I didn't panic at all and I had expected I would.

So I went upstairs in the dark. And I think, considering the fact that I couldn't see what I was packing, I did a fair job, because I got everything in the suitcase and we all rushed out to the car, Emma as well. Emma sat in her usual place in the back, and when we arrived at the hospital she had to stay in the car because she wasn't allowed inside the building. I suppose the nurses must have thought it odd because while I lay in the labour ward and Don sat by my side, the main part of our conversation was about Emma—if you can call a series of fragmented remarks 'conversation'.

'Is Emma all right?' I said between contractions.

'I'll go and have another look at her,' said Don, and I heard his footsteps receding down the long corridor. And I waited for him to come back.

'It's a bit cold out there,' he said on his return. 'I've given her an extra blanket, and had the engine going to warm her up.'

'Oh, thank goodness for that,' I said. I think Don split his time evenly between Emma and me while I was having the baby. I very much wanted a little girl. Don didn't mind either way. But I wanted a little girl, and that was just what she turned out to be. We decided to call her Kerensa, an old Cornish name in Don's family.

Two days later I was coming home in the ambulance, and, although I knew I should have felt wildly happy, I was anything but. My concern about Emma had started to weigh on me again and I was apprehensive as I sat there, Kerensa on my lap, getting nearer and nearer home. What would Emma think? I was bringing a stranger into the house. Somebody that Emma didn't know. Somebody that would need a lot of my attention, a lot of my time. I felt a traitor. I felt, after all Emma had meant to me and still meant now she was twelve, as if I was somehow doing wrong. It may sound incredible, but I didn't want to take the baby home. It was as if I was pushing Emma aside for something else, something better. I didn't know what to do. And when you have a baby, you don't love it instantly—I didn't

Zimba

Ming

Holly

Sheila, Emma, Kerensa

Buttons

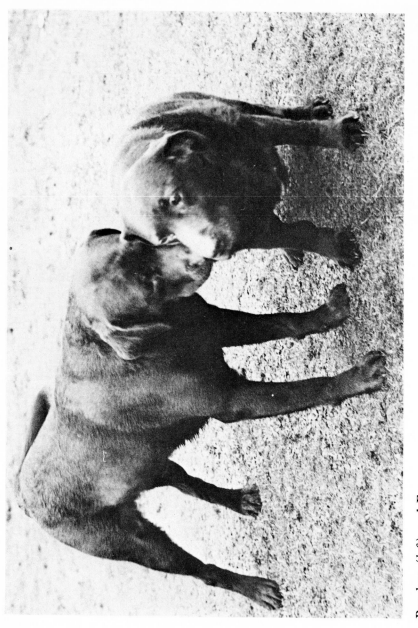

Bracken (*left*) and Emma

anyway, and I am sure many mothers feel like this. The baby, much as I wanted her, was a stranger, someone I had to get to know and love. And at that time in the ambulance, Emma meant far more to me than a baby could.

When we got to the house, I asked the ambulance driver if he would mind carrying Kerensa in for me. At least if he did that Emma would not be put off by me actually carrying a stranger, and we could say hello to each other before she had to accept the new being. And that is how it was. The door opened, and there was that loving chocolate-brown shape waiting, tail wagging and eyes saying, 'Here you are. Where have you been? What have you been doing?' I bent down to her. 'Hello, sausage,' I said, and she gave snuffles of delight as the ambulance driver slipped in behind me and handed the baby to Don.

In fact, I needn't have worried about Emma accepting the baby. The older Kerensa grew, the more Emma took her as truly a part of the family. At the same time I made sure that, in Emma's thoughts at least, I made more of her than the baby. She got far more titbits than she had ever done before: the long-standing rule had to go by the board, although I still had to be careful that she didn't put on too much weight. But it didn't seem fair to Emma to see this new little creature being fed all the time and for her to get nothing. So she got extra bowls of milk, and extra biscuits. Also, and more comically, squeaky rubber toys sent as gifts to Kerensa inevitably ended up, sooner or later, in Emma's paws.

Ming, on the other hand, was rather jealous of Kerensa when she first arrived. So every time I fed the baby, Ming had to come and sit on my knee. With her there and Emma at my feet, I had more than enough to cope with. But all the animals came to accept Kerensa eventually. More than that, in time, Emma quite obviously became fond of Kerensa. I don't think she would have liked me to know that, but one day I caught her out. Kerensa was in her pram outside the back door and Emma was pottering about the garden. Someone came round to the back of the house and, instead of coming to the door and knocking, they stopped to speak to Kerensa. I have never seen Emma react so quickly. She raced from the bottom of the garden, barking furiously. She got to the pram, hackles raised, and—so unlike her normal sedate self—actually snarled at the woman who was bending over the pram. She, in turn, was so frightened she took off immediately in the direction of the gate. Emma had given the game away. She really cared for Kerensa!

Later, Emma suddenly developed an even closer relationship with Kerensa. It coincided precisely with the time that Kerensa was old enough to sit and eat biscuits on her own. Emma discovered immediately that nothing would have been easier than to take a biscuit out of that little hand. But to give Emma her due, greedy as she may be, she would never do that. She used to sit and look furtively at Kerensa, occasionally looking away to pretend that she was not in the slightest bit interested. And, if she happened to catch my eye, a look would spread over her face that suggested she was successfully grappling with the temptations of Satan himself. I almost began to think I could see a halo beginning to form over those velvety brown ears.

I believe that Kerensa must, from the beginning, have thought that Emma was a part of me, because we were always together. When she started to talk I was not called 'Mummy'. I was called 'Emma'. And Emma was called 'Emma' and most other things, too. When she was a young baby and I had to get up and feed her in the middle of the night, Emma came too and watched all the proceedings. It was as if she *had* to get up. I don't think she was particularly keen on being dragged out of her basket in the small hours, but if I was doing it, then she considered it her duty as well. No doubt in time she could have told me how to make a bottle and change a nappy.

And whenever Kerensa went out in the pram, Emma naturally went too. It was surprising how quickly she adapted to the fact that there was a pram in front of me. Emma elected to keep on the left side and walk a bit out from the pram. At these times it was Kerensa I felt sorry for, however. I still hadn't got the hang of going up and down kerbs, and having a pram to push made it all the more difficult. Often I wouldn't anticipate a kerb, the pram would leap down in front of me, Kerensa would get a shaking and Emma would look at me as if to say, '*Do* be careful.'

Still, Kerensa survived. I wish I could say that in the early

78

part of 1977 we were as happy about another, more serious, aspect of her existence. From the moment I knew I was pregnant I had thought about it; so had Don, although he rarely said anything about it. Would our baby inherit the family eye defect that had so altered the lives of my mother, my father, my brother and myself? I was convinced in an odd way— perhaps it all went back to Alasdair Macdonald and the circumstances of his strange prophecy—that any baby I had would have perfect sight. But I knew Don was worried. I also knew that if I had not made optimism my defence, I would have been as worried as he was.

There was no way of telling, short of a thorough examination, whether, even if her vision seemed right at the outset, it would remain so. We had to wait six weeks before Mr Shearing, the specialist who had performed my operation and given me sight, could make that examination.

One day his secretary rang to say that Mr Shearing would see Kerensa the following Tuesday. As I put the phone down I remembered the words of this kind and understanding specialist when he had said he would operate on me: 'I don't work miracles, lassie.'

I knew that Don, at least, would be hoping for nothing short of a miracle on that next Tuesday.

CHAPTER SEVEN

OVER THE INTERVENING days Don became progressively quieter, strangely withdrawn, and tense; not at all his easy-going and cheerful self. It was as if there was a spring inside him, being wound up tighter and tighter, nearly to breaking-point.

I tried talking to him about his anxiety, but it was no good. I tried getting his mind away from thoughts of Kerensa's eye-sight, getting him to talk about his painting, the hobby which took up most of his spare time, but that was of no use either. I knew, equally, that my telling him I felt convinced she would have perfect vision would also be useless. All attempts at conversation led inevitably back to the only certainty he would entertain: the uncertainty of Kerensa's ability to see, and the fact that Mr Shearing would dispel all doubts—one way or another.

It was like living with someone who was incessantly spinning a coin in his mind, and when Tuesday came I was relieved even at the mere action of us all getting in the car for the journey. I was beyond thinking of the outcome, or its possible implications. Emma curled up on her seat and went to sleep. I had Kerensa in my arms. We put a bottle in my bag in case she was upset by Mr Shearing looking at her eyes.

As we went along I looked out of the window and saw the trees and fields beside the motorway. Even though they were leafless and bleak they held some sort of magic for me because, in reverse, this was the journey I had made coming back from the hospital the very first time that I could see. Even eighteen months later it still made my heart beat faster to go on that same journey. But there was one great difference: this time we went along in almost complete silence.

At last we reached Mr Shearing's. 'I'm glad he likes Emma,' I said to Don as we got out of the car and I put her lead on.

'There aren't many specialists who would let a dog in their surgery, are there?'

'No,' said Don.

'I mean, he's always so pleased to see Emma, isn't he? I'm sure he'd be disappointed if we didn't bring her.'

'Yes, I expect he would,' said Don.

I remembered so well that strangely clean and antiseptic smell mixed with floor polish. I decided not to bother trying to make conversation. We sat in the waiting-room. Kerensa was on my knee and Emma sat at my feet. I tried to lose myself in the open fire burning in a huge fireplace which took up almost a quarter of the room. I watched the flames and was fascinated. I loved watching and making pictures in the fire, and imagining all sorts of things being there.

I came out of my dream when the door opened and Mr Shearing came in, greeting me as he always had: 'Hello lassie, hello there. Come on in.'

At that moment Don suddenly came across the waiting-room and took Kerensa off my lap. I knew how he felt: somehow if he held her, everything would be all right. Emma and I followed him into the surgery. Don hardly said a word to Mr Shearing.

'I see Emma's well,' said Mr Shearing over his shoulder; and, when we were all in the surgery: 'Now, let's have a look at this new little bundle.'

Don held tightly on to Kerensa as Mr Shearing took his various instruments and started peering into her eyes. Don was trembling and looked desperately apprehensive. I sat looking across at him, wanting to say, 'Don't worry, I know she'll be all right—because we love each other. Perhaps she won't be able to see, but we would still love each other and any difficulties can be surmounted that way.'

'Hum,' Mr Shearing kept saying infuriatingly. 'Hum . . . yes . . . hm . . .' Apart from that there was a silence in which I could hear him breathing, and the clock ticking, and an occasional sound from Kerensa.

'Hmm . . .' said Mr Shearing again. 'Well, you look a nice, healthy little girl.' And there was a further silence as he went over and put his instruments away.

Don cleared his throat. 'What's the verdict?' I had never

heard his voice tremble like that before. Mr Shearing came back across the room and patted Don on the shoulder. Then he smiled. 'It's all right, laddie,' he said. 'She'll be all right. She's got away with it.'

Instantly Don's face was a sunburst of relief, happiness and pride, all at once. 'Thank God,' he said. 'Thank you Mr Shearing. Isn't it *wonderful*?'

'I knew she would be able to see,' I said. 'I just did. Oh, thank you Mr Shearing.'

'Ah well . . . you're both looking well. You've got no troubles with that little girl.'

It was the way he always, almost self-consciously, brushed aside any thanks. I was surprised he didn't start talking about Nottingham Forest Football Club, as he had when I thanked him after my operation. Instead he turned his attention to Emma, bent down, and patted her.

'Well, how are you, old girl? How's retirement suiting you? Has she been taking you out for walks? It looks as if she's been feeding you well, anyway, lass.' Then he looked up at me.

'How are the contact lenses going, lassie?'

'Oh, marvellous. I'd never go back to glasses.'

'Good. I wondered if you'd get on all right with those soft contact lenses.'

And with that he showed us out into the February sunshine. We stood there for a moment saying goodbye on the pavement and I realized, much as I had been convinced that everything would turn out for the best, the sun was confirmation of our relief. At the same time, I thought: And it will never go dark for Kerensa. At that moment, perversely, she began to cry.

In the weeks that followed the sense of relief changed into something quite different, something that could never have existed when all I had was a dogged private conviction that Kerensa would be able to see properly. Sight to me was like an extra faculty that had suddenly been grafted on to my being; now Kerensa's sight brought another dimension. I had not had a sighted childhood, but now I was able to share hers and it was an utterly joyful experience.

It gave me yet another fresh view of the importance of sight, its part in discovery for a child and in the child's growing awareness of everything in the world around. Sight—as I had only recently learnt, as an adult—augmented touch and smell and hearing, but only through sight were most new experiences exciting and beautiful. When I give Kerensa a biscuit, she feels it, she smells it, she shakes it to see if it will rattle like a toy; but above all, before she bites it, she looks at it so that every piece of information about that biscuit is stored in her brain.

I know, of course, part of the excitement of coming into a new world visually, but how much more exciting it must be for a baby. Every sound, every smell, every touch—they are all new and have to be investigated visually. There are so many things, I realize now more than ever, that a blind child will miss in life, and so much education is lost because the visual learning is cut off. I will never forget the pleasure I saw on Kerensa's face when she first saw a bird fly over her in her pram. It was a miracle to her. As a baby, I would never have seen such a thing. And that is why I realize now that birds, apart from their sounds, had no place in my consciousness before I could see. I had no direct means of knowing they fly about the sky, or perch in trees, or hop on the lawn. Kerensa knows from the beginning, just as she will know from the beginning that every tree is different and that grass is not simply green, but every shade of green. I hope I shall be able to bring her up in a way that ensures she never loses that first fascination with life, and, particularly, the appreciation of the visual side of life.

Bringing up Kerensa intrigued me and occupied me most of my time, especially at the crawling stage—as I need tell no parent—although for me there was an extra interest in the way Emma dealt with this now-mobile object at her own eye level. She was very patient, even when, before I had got the message across that it was not allowed, her tail and ears were used as painful handgrips to an unsteady standing position. Apart from all this, I was also finding time to write a book about Emma and myself. And I had other ambitions as well.

I had always wanted a cattery. Not (at first, anyway) a commercial boarding cattery, but a place where I could look after the kittens of my own Siamese cats which I had sold to people, to make sure that they would come back and be well looked after when their owners had to go away. Ming, still as wise and mischievous as ever, was and still is with me, joined by Hera, a Red Point, and Rahny, a Tortie Point and, from time to time, their offspring, so quite a variety of colours were stalking about the house.

When I was able to see, I was appalled at some of the catteries I went to. I would not have trusted them with a pet goldfish, let alone my Siamese cats. One in particular left a deep and black impression on my mind. The cats were kept in tiny cages, about the size of rabbit hutches, perhaps two foot by two to be generous. They were lined along the wall of a long shed, stacked one on top of the other. When I went in there and saw about fifty cats, all looking at me from these tiny pens, I could have wept. To think that the owners would leave them here, all cooped up, while they went on holiday! I resolved there and then that a cat I had bred would never, if it could be avoided, have to go to such a nightmarish place.

This led me on to consider how to be independent of other catteries, and I thought a good deal about what would be ideal surroundings for a cat coming to stay. And eventually I designed, with loving care, a cattery to occupy the space in the garden behind the surgery where there was plenty of room, and work began on building it. My cat-houses were cabins on legs, about six foot by six, with ladders up to them and a little cat-door, a shelf for the cats to stretch out on and sun themselves, a heated bed and their own light. I had all the houses double-glazed and fibreglass lined. Possibly the cats might even think themselves more comfortable in one of those than our own house, which is certainly not fibreglass lined and double-glazed. And each cat, with its own house, has a run which is quite large so that they don't feel hemmed in; they have lots of room in which to move about, and feel free. I think this is very important when a cat moves to a strange place as it won't be so scared if it has plenty of space around it for its own use.

One day, soon after we had our first boarders, Don came out of the surgery. 'I've got a patient in and her daughter can't see,' he said. 'She goes away to that special school in Coventry. Apparently the lass loves animals and the mother wants to know if she could bring her round to look at the cats and have a look at the cattery—and she wants to meet Emma as well.'

'Yes, fine,' I said. 'Tell her to give us a ring and let us know when she's coming.'

Susan, who was fourteen, came round about a week later. She was not totally blind as Don had thought, but she couldn't see very much.

'Come up the garden,' I told her. 'I'll show you the cat-houses.'

I turned round to make sure that she could find her own way. She was managing. She was a nice-looking girl with glasses, in a blazer covered with all sorts of badges. I could see her peering, trying to identify the vague visual images in front of her to make sure that she wouldn't bump into anything or fall over. I didn't want to fuss round her. I knew all too well what it was like to be fourteen and not to be able to see much, with people trying to drag you and push you and making everything worse.

My mind went back to when I was fourteen, quite obsessed then, as now, with animals and particularly dogs, and how I managed to get a weekend job at a local boarding kennels. But, unlike Susan, I had covered up the fact that I couldn't see properly. One Saturday I was exercising a big Alsatian in the field and he slipped his lead. I had no idea where he had gone and was panic-stricken. In my mind I could hear the screech of brakes as he got out on to the road and was run over—all because I wouldn't admit I couldn't see. I waved his lead and collar-chain and shouted myself hoarse—and to my astonishment I at last heard him galumphing back towards me and I had him safely into his collar again, just hoping no one had witnessed me in my secret near-blindness trying to cope.

'Have you any pets?' I asked. I was trying to guide her by my voice as well as being interested in her pets.

'I've got a rabbit,' she said, 'but I love dogs and cats.'

'Have you seen Siamese before? Oh, mind the gate. That's right, this way.'

'Thanks,' she said. I shut the gate behind us. 'No, I haven't seen Siamese, but I've heard about them. They're nice cats aren't they?'

'Well, I think so,' I said.

'Have you got any in at the moment?'

'Only my own Siamese up at the top here, Zimba.'

'Have you got only one?'

'No, I've got four,' I said, 'but the other three are females and they live in their own place in the house. I'm afraid Zimba has to live outside, because he's a stud cat.'

'Does that make a difference?' she asked.

'Well, yes, it does rather. If I let him in the house he would be trying to mate everything in sight. Anyway, come and look at his outside house. It's not as bad as it seems when I say he lives outside. This way, in this gate,' I told her. I opened the gate. 'Here he is, in here.'

Zimba came dashing out, miaowing and climbing up Susan's legs.

'Ow! He's got sharp claws.'

'Yes, you'll have to watch him. Pick him up. He's all right. He's quite friendly.'

I watched her putting her hands down to make sure that she'd got hold of him properly. And all this time, looking at Susan, I could see myself, the self of years ago. It was unnerving. But I know that if I had been Susan, I would have liked somebody to treat me as an equal and a normal human being, and I'd got to keep remembering that, because I was on the other side of the fence now. Zimba had curled himself round Susan's neck, and was purring in her ear.

'I wish we could have some more animals,' she said, 'but we haven't room. Do you think I could come up and help you sometimes with the cats?'

When she asked that, a lot of thoughts rushed through my mind all at once. I thought: She can't see. I can't let her help me with the cats. She wouldn't know if they got out of the gate. And if I'd got somebody's kitten in for boarding, what would I do if she lost it? I couldn't take the risk. And even if I asked her to sweep a cat-house out, she wouldn't see if it was clean. What can I say to her?

And then I remembered myself again, years ago, as a schoolgirl. I remembered what it was like to be nearly blind, what it was like when I went for weekend jobs at kennels, desperately hoping they wouldn't know I couldn't see and desperately wanting to help with the animals. How could I think critically

of Susan after all those years of being on the other side myself?
And of complaining that sighted people would not accept me?

'Yes, of course you can help me,' I said. 'I'd be very glad of
some help from somebody. Come round whenever you like.
Are you going to come in and see the other cats?—you'd better
get to know them if you're coming to help.'

'Oh, can I? Please,' she said. She followed me down the
garden and into the house. She was thrilled to see the rest of the
cats, and Emma as well. 'You're Emma are you? I've heard
about you. Did you say she was chocolate brown?'

'That's right.'

'She just looks dark to me . . . by the way I shan't be able to
come for a bit because I'm away at school. But I'll come at half
term which is in five weeks' time.'

'Fine,' I said. 'I'll look forward to seeing you. Where do you
go to school?'

'In Coventry.'

'Do you like it?'

'Oh, it's all right I suppose.'

And that brought back more memories to me: how unjust it
seemed to take children from their parents and put them in a
special school because they had a handicap. And how lucky I
had been that my mother insisted on me trying my best at an
ordinary sighted school where I could live at home and not have
to leave friends behind at the beginning of every term.

I am glad that I asked Susan to come and help me. It proved
a lucky stroke. She is still with me and very happy. She has
become a tremendous help, and she is, I am certain, more
trustworthy than any sighted child of her age, because from the
very beginning she took things responsibly. I think she knew she
had to do a good job—just as I did at her age—and always aim
to do better than a sighted person. If you are blind, you have to
do that in order to win: the world, which wants to ignore you
anyway, will forget you soon enough if you ever stop competing.

So my private cattery went along fairly smoothly. There were
occasional problems with the cats but, on the whole, I found the
owners more of a headache than their pets. Two of my regular
visitors were Siamese from my friend Ann. The first time they
arrived she had already inspected where they would be living

for a fortnight while she was on holiday. We put them in their pen, settled them down, and I thought that was the end of it. I was wrong.

Ann came back with me into the house. 'Now then,' she said, 'I've brought all their instructions for you.'

'Instructions? What instructions?' I said. 'They're Siamese, and, after all, I bred them. I think I know what they'll eat and everything.'

'Well, yes, I'm sure you do Sheila, but I thought I would just leave the odd instruction to make sure you wouldn't have any worries while I'm away.'

The 'odd instruction' turned out to be four sheets of foolscap typed paper, carefully filed in a perspex cover. She took it out of her bag.

'And,' she said, as if that was not enough for me to study over the next fortnight, 'there are two ointments. One's for Tiger and the other's for Whisky. Then there are two sets of pills. It tells you about these on my instructions, but Whisky has to have one pill in the morning and one pill after her supper at night. And Tiger should have a pill every third day—unless he sneezes—and then I give him two a day . . . oh, and I forgot. Here are the eardrops . . .'

'Eardrops?' I said in astonishment. 'What's the matter with their ears?'

'Oh, well, nothing actually. But it's just *in case*.' She leaned forward earnestly. 'I always like to take precautions. You never know, do you?'

'Well, they're not going to catch anything here,' I said.

'Oh, I wouldn't suggest for a moment that I thought they might, but it's *just in case* . . . and I'd be so grateful if you'd follow the instruction on sheet number three. Paragraph two.'

'Oh, I will,' I assured her, by now quite bemused. 'I will.'

'Now. Would you take special note of this little bit about Whisky. Page one, top of the page. Paragraph one.'

I looked at the typewritten sheet, as directed.

'Whisky is a very strange Siamese,' said Ann, while I was thinking that it was not Whisky that was a little bit odd. 'She likes to be made a fuss of, but she must have four feet on the ground.'

'What do you mean, "four feet on the ground"?'

'Well, she doesn't like to be picked up. Not at all. But she does like to be made a fuss of, as long as you leave *all* her feet on the ground.'

'Oh, all right. I'll make sure I do that. What about Tiger? Does he like fussing with four feet on the ground?'

'No. No, he doesn't. Tiger's very different. It's all in my notes. He likes to sit on your shoulder. So if you'd go in, in the morning when you give them their breakfast, and just let him sit on your shoulder for a few minutes, that will make him content for the rest of the day.'

She began fastening her bag and doing up her coat. 'Well, I'll leave you to it, but with my instructions' (she tapped them meaningfully and fixed me with a beady look), 'I'm sure there's nothing you won't know how to cope with.'

'I'm sure,' I said rather weakly, and then: 'By the way, have you a phone number, just in case?'

'No,' she said, 'I am going off to Spain.'

'Are you sure you're quite happy about them?' I said, expecting her to ring every night even if she had been off to Australia.

'Oh, *quite* sure,' she said, sweeping to the front door. She paused on the step. 'You won't forget the eye ointment, will you,' she said as a parting shot.

Simon was another interesting visitor, and 'interesting' is only one adjective he deserved. Simon belonged to another friend, Mrs Blake, a slightly overpowering lady with a voice that boomed out at you. Her Simon was just about the most spoilt of all the spoilt Siamese I had ever met.

'Ooh, my poor darling!' said Mrs Blake in reverberating tones as she brought Simon in and saw where he was going to live. 'I don't know how you're going to manage without Mummy.' Somehow the line was given the kind of treatment Shakespeare would have approved of. She followed up by kissing him lavishly, all over his nose. Simon, to give him his due, didn't seem to be too appreciative of that. Cats don't much like being kissed—certainly not by humans, although perhaps another cat is OK.

'Don't worry, Mrs Blake,' I assured her. 'I'll look after him. He's got his heated bed on and there's plenty of food ready for him. I don't think you need worry. I'm sure he'll settle—all the others do.'

She turned to me. 'Ooh . . . but you haven't had my little poppet before!' she boomed. 'He'll miss Mummy taking him to bed. Oh, you poor darling, you'll have to sleep all on your own! Where will he have his food?'

'In his house,' I said. 'They all have their food bowls in their houses.'

'Ooh, I'm not sure he'll approve of that. He always sits at the table with me. He likes to eat his dinner off a china plate. I personally use Dresden. Oh, he will miss that. Now, he likes lightly-poached fish for breakfast. Won't touch anything else. I've tried him with bacon, but he doesn't seem to like the rind, you know. And for dinner, I might boil him a kidney. And he always has fresh rabbit for tea. Then, depending what Mummy has for supper, he shares it with me.'

'Don't worry,' I said. 'I've got all that down.' At the same time I didn't bother to tell her that Simon would be getting used to chicken for breakfast not fish, lightly-poached or otherwise, and was also in for other amendments to his diet.

After Mrs Blake had departed, I realized that her influence over Simon had gone a little too far. Nothing I could do would make him come round to my way of thinking. I don't normally mind if cats spit at me, or growl, because at least I know where I am with them. Cats only behave like that out of fear. As soon as they are used to you walking round their run and become accustomed to your voice, they come to you for affection.

But Simon wouldn't come anywhere near me. He sat on the roof of his cabin all day, and every time I opened his front gate I felt his open hostility. He hated me. The look in his eyes appeared full of a baleful hope that I would drop dead. But at least he ate everything I put in front of him and, in fact, he put on weight while he was with me. The diet was obviously better for him than the lightly-poached fish, etc.

Simon was with me for a fortnight and never, ever could I actually touch him. But one day I went into the run to serve his evening meal and I was not as careful as usual. I normally ducked to be out of reach of his perch on the top of the roof, and put his dinner down in his house. Only this time I felt the hate was not quite as strong as it had been previously.

How wrong I was. I walked in, my head level with the roof, within about six inches of Simon. He lashed out at my face, just missing my eye and scratching skin off my cheek. I was so furious I just stood there and stamped my feet. I hardly knew what to do with him. In what Simon obviously saw as a competition between us, I had lost, and I had never encountered that sort of thing before. After a few days I have always been on the best terms with the cats I've promised to look after.

I took Simon in when Mrs Blake went away again. The only thing that made me take him was the thought that if I didn't, he might go to a commercial cattery where they simply wouldn't understand his ways—which are worse than those of a spoilt child.

Yet, despite occasional characters such as Simon and despite the fact that running even a little private cattery is hard and often dirty work, I loved every minute of it. I knew from the beginning that I loved being outside and being with animals, so much so that it was not long before I realized that nothing less than a full-scale boarding cattery, and kennels for dogs, would satisfy me.

Sadly, the local council objected to me looking after other people's cats, as they were of the opinion that it was a business. Having tried to convince them for over a year that no way was I making any money, I gave up the fight, and since then I have been unable to board even the kittens I have bred. All this made me more determined to find a place in the country where I could realize my ambition.

CHAPTER EIGHT

DURING THE TIME I had my limited Utopia—the cattery I had already built—I sometimes used to think perhaps I was insane to want that kind of life on an even bigger scale. It could be freezing, wet, and highly unpleasant cleaning those cat-houses out, even with Susan's help when she came along. Of course, there were other forms of help (Emma), and, sometimes, hindrance (Kerensa). Emma is not the sort of dog to sit about and do nothing. Since my operation, and she was no longer guiding me, she obviously had to find other responsibilities so she could still feel an essential part of us. Emma somehow ensured that everything in the house revolved round her. She found different roles in life, things she knew she was needed for, and one of them was waiting outside the cat-runs when I was feeding the boarders. She clearly felt that it was her place to sit outside those doors and stay there until I came out again. What also entered into this, no doubt, was the fact that when I did come out I usually brought all the food bowls; and, since some cats never quite finished up their meals, Emma liked to ensure that every plate was clean even before it went to be washed up. So perhaps that lay behind the desire for responsibility. But there was another reason. When Kerensa reached the toddling stage she always came with me as well. I didn't mind that because I could keep an eye on her and see (because she had soon become fond of animals) that she didn't pick up any cats who weren't used to her. And here Emma, standing guard, was an extra pair of eyes. She knew she played her part in looking after Kerensa.

I didn't realize, however, how fast Kerensa was growing: upwards, that is. But one day it was brought home to me. I discovered she could undo the bolts on the cat-runs. She was playing out in the garden, and I was in the kitchen washing up. I didn't know where Emma was, but I thought she was in the garden watching Kerensa. Suddenly I heard her barking.

Normally she does not bark a great deal—only occasionally when people come to the door, in order to let us know someone is there. For the most part the drive is very busy with patients coming to and from Don's surgery. There is an iron gate between the garden and the surgery so Emma can see all the patients but she knows they have a right to be there and she never barks at them. So I wondered why she was barking in the back garden.

'Emma!' I called. I was answered by more furious barking. 'Emma, what's the matter?' She didn't come to the back door, but simply barked even more.

I put my tea-towel down and went into the garden. Emma was standing by the cat-runs.

'What is it Emma?' I said. She barked again. Then I looked. There was a gate open and Kerensa was standing there with a kitten clutched in her little hands, giggling, laughing and dancing about saying, 'Baby kitten, baby kitten.'

'Kerensa! Have you let the mum out?' I looked into the cat-house. It was empty. Mum had gone. What was I to do? Emma stood there wagging her tail in front of the open gate. 'Where is she, Emma? Where's she gone?'

Emma immediately and with a great sense of purpose led me along the side of the garden. And there, sitting licking her paws between two rose bushes, was the kitten's mum.

'Oh, Sheena, thank goodness you haven't gone far.' I scooped her up and put her back in the cat-run with her kitten. Now I shall have to padlock the gates, I thought.

'You're a naughty girl, Kerensa,' I said. But when Emma bounded up, pushing her nose into my hand and wagging her tail so her whole backside moved, I said, 'And you're a *good* girl.' I knew what had happened. Emma had seen Kerensa undoing the gate, had *known* it was not the right thing to do if I was not there and had barked to let me know.

Some time before this I had a growing preoccupation beyond the cats, Emma and Kerensa. It was my first book *Emma and I*, on which I had been working increasingly hard, putting the final touches and making revisions. Earlier in the year I had been thrilled when it had been accepted for publication. That had been a tremendous moment in all our lives, but I was not prepared for the reception it had when it came out in the autumn of that year. It went to the top of the bestseller list—and immediately I had visions that were more than dreams. Might we, after all, be able to afford a new and really full-size boarding cattery and kennels?

Following the publication of the book Emma and I embarked on a non-stop whirl of tours round the country, making appearances at bookshops and autographing copies. In addition, we had all sorts of invitations to speak on radio and appear on television shows, and in each instance Emma, in her own way—and very appropriately—nearly always managed in some way to steal the show.

The very first appearance we made was with Russell Harty for London Weekend Television. Lynn Silver, the programme organizer, rang up to confirm details.

'You will be bringing Emma, won't you?' she said.

'Oh yes, of course. I never go anywhere without her.'

'Oh, that's splendid.'

I voiced her thoughts for her: 'You mean if I didn't bring Emma, you really wouldn't want *me*, would you?'

She laughed, but I knew there was some truth in this.

Don, Susan (Don's daughter from his first marriage), Emma and I set off for London for the show. We were all immensely excited. I was so excited, in fact, that when we got to Nottingham Midland Station and the train came in, Emma and I were first on it and it was not until I was actually in my seat that I suddenly realized that I had not got the dress I had bought specially for the show. I had spent hours going round the Nottingham shops before I found what I wanted: a long dark green velvet dress—actually a two-piece—with a blouse under the top. And, just as the train was about to pull out with only one stop between there and St Pancras, that dress was lying in a carrier-bag on a seat on the platform.

'Don!' I said. 'I've left the carrier with the dress in it on the seat.'

He dashed off the train, colliding with people still stowing their luggage and settling in their seats, sprinted down the platform, and just got back aboard as the whistle was blowing.

'What on earth made you do that?' he said breathlessly.
'What would you have done?'

I had no answer to that one, but I spent the rest of the two hours going down to London permutating a small nightmare of arriving without anything to wear beyond what I had travelled in.

London Weekend Television turned out to be a skyscraper building: something which I still have not got used to. To look up at a skyscraper, with the clouds going past and making it seem to move, makes me feel dizzy. We walked in through the main doors, and I had to close my eyes and pretend I was walking into an ordinary building.

Lynn Silver met us and we were taken up in the lift, with me, once again, trying not to think of how many storeys high we were. We arrived in her office and I didn't dare look out of the window.

I met Russell Harty only very briefly before the show. He said that he had read the book and would be asking me questions going through the book chronologically. Then he sprang rather a surprise.

'I don't want you to come on with Emma,' he said.

'Oh, why not? I don't think I *could* come on without her. After all she's at least the other half of the book.'

'No,' he said, 'it's not that. I'd like her to sit with your husband in the audience. Then, about halfway through, I'll get you to call Emma to come on and sit by your chair. Do you think she'd do that?'

I didn't much like the idea. 'Oh, she'll come all right. But I must tell you I don't fancy the idea of walking on by myself.' It was strange, but in moments like that, sighted as I was, I still very much needed Emma to give me confidence. I felt that if she was there by my side nothing could go wrong.

Then I asked: 'Are there any stairs to come down?'

'Yes, you have to come down a flight of stairs, but don't worry—we'll show you them before the show starts and you can see how you go.' I felt I needed Emma even more when he told me that. This was something I had still not become accustomed to with sight: negotiating steps I didn't know.

Although I didn't get Emma's guidance as strongly through a lead as I used to through the harness, she had always helped me with unfamiliar steps back in Nottingham. I still judged from her pace how far up or down we had to go and I relied on that, rather than trust the message from my eyes to my brain which did not always give the right distance.

So I immediately dreaded the idea of going on alone, down stairs.

Lynn took me behind the set. 'Now don't worry about the stairs,' she said. 'They're not rickety or anything, and they're all level.'

We had a little rehearsal, and it was not very successful. The steps were curved down from the back of the set on to a carpeted plinth where there were two seats and a table. I tried to memorize how many steps there were, and that there was a turning halfway down. With lights glaring at me and an audience looking at me, to say nothing of unseen but watching eyes at their television screens, I knew it was not going to be easy. I thought: Well, you're just going to have to go back to the old times when you didn't have Emma. You'll just have to feel with your feet.

As the show started, I sat alone at the back of the set. Emma had gone into the audience and was curled up under the seat between Don and Susan. I was due to appear last. I was very nervous. I saw on a monitor what was happening on the show and a few seconds before my entrance Lynn took me to the top of the steps behind the set. I don't know how a paratrooper feels before he jumps from the aircraft, but I think I have a good idea.

'Don't worry,' said Lynn, 'you'll be all right.'

'I'll have to be,' I said.

I heard Russell Harty say my name—which was my cue—and the applause, and out I went into the dazzling light. I just couldn't see the steps at all. I was also conscious of how nervous I was. I had to feel with my feet: no, there was not a step yet. Then, there it was. Help! I nearly missed that one. The viewers might not have seen it, but I was shaking. But I managed to get down that flight of stairs, on to the plinth, and once I had sat down I breathed the most enormous sigh of relief.

Russell Harty commented on the book, and as soon as we started talking I forgot my nerves and then felt encouraged as the audience laughed at the little things I told them about Emma.

Suddenly, Russell said that Emma was in the audience, and would she come if I called her? I stood and called, 'Emma! Come on, there's a good girl!' And she immediately came running on to the stage and wagged her tail excitedly round me before settling down beside my chair. Russell went on asking questions, and I noticed after a time that Emma had disappeared. I looked on the other side of my chair and there she was. I had no idea why she had done that. Perhaps she had not been comfortable.

But as soon as the show finished, one of the cameramen came up to me.

'I must tell you,' he said, 'I'd already heard a lot about Emma and what a fabulous dog she is, and I must admit I really didn't believe that a dog could be so clever. But I believe it all now, I really do.'

'Why's that?' I asked.

'Well,' he said, 'when you called her up on to the set, she went round one side of your chair and she was completely out of camera—I couldn't get her at all, and I forgot she was just a dog and started waving her over to the other side. And do you know what? She got up and went round the chair and sat just where I wanted her to.'

I laughed. 'Well, I told you Emma was exceptional.'

'My word, you're right,' he said, patting Emma, who looked up at him with an expression that said: 'Well, of course, you should never have doubted my intelligence in the first place.'

Later, Emma became very tired of the whole business of radio and television studios. Certainly she took everything in her stride. When everyone used to come up and pat and stroke her, she wagged her tail at them and then just settled down. It didn't matter what the programme was, or how important— she simply lay down by my feet and went off to sleep. Most of the interviewers assumed this was Emma's way, but one was not suited at all, or at least his producer didn't seem to be. One reason for Emma going to sleep in front of the cameras was, of course, the studio lighting: hot even for humans, but doubly so for a dog.

We had been asked to appear on Anglia Television, and Emma curled up as soon as the programme was under way and took no further interest in the proceedings. We did the interview, which lasted about four minutes, and I answered all the questions. We finished and the interviewer said, 'Right. That's fine. Thank you.' Emma roused herself and we were just walking out of the studio when he called me back.

'The producer wants us to do it again,' he said.

'Why?' I asked. 'What did I say wrong? Didn't I give the right answers?'

'No, that was OK. You were perfectly all right. But he didn't like the look of the dog.'

'Didn't like the look of the dog? What do you mean?'

'Well, she didn't do anything, did she? She was just lying there.'

'What does he expect? Somersaults?'

'No, I don't think so . . .' By this time I was rather cross on Emma's behalf.

'Well, ask the producer what he wants,' I said.

The interviewer disappeared and came back a minute later.

'I think what he would like is for her to sort of sit up and look round or do something.'

I decided there and then that Emma was not going under the lights again. She was getting on in years, and going on tour wasn't a strain for her only because I made sure it wasn't. I made certain she had her meals and water at the proper times and that she got lots of comforts, and I was certainly not going to allow her to do cartwheels or sit up and look interesting for any producer anywhere.

And whether the viewers liked it or not, Emma was fast asleep when that interview finally appeared on the screen.

One morning a letter arrived and I really could not believe my eyes when I opened it. Inside was an invitation for me to speak at the Woman of the Year luncheon at the Savoy Hotel in London. Just to have been invited to be there would have been beyond my wildest dreams, but to be invited to speak as well!

98

I called upstairs to Don, and ran up to the bathroom where he was shaving. 'Don! Don! Look at this!' I pushed the letter in front of his nose, and he said, 'Steady. You'll get shaving cream all over it.'

I was too excited to tell him about it, and I wanted him to read it for himself. So, with his face still lathered, he read the card.

'Do you think they've made a mistake?' I said.

'No. They can't have. It says "Sheila Hocken" plain enough.'

I was not really convinced, so I wrote back and accepted immediately just in case they changed their minds. I also put a note in to make sure the invitation was to Emma as well as myself.

'What will you do if they won't have Emma?' Don asked after I had posted my reply.

'I wouldn't go.'

'Really? Do you mean that? Would you really turn down an invitation as important as that if you can't go with Emma?'

'Well, I'm certainly not going without her.'

I was delighted, therefore, when a further letter arrived to say that Emma, naturally, was included in the invitation, and would I speak about loyalty? Well, that was a nice easy subject, because I felt that loyalty was something both Emma and I knew all about.

I didn't really want to go down to London on my own, but since it was an all-woman affair (which included Emma!) they would certainly not allow Don in. But he said he would go down with me and arranged to have lunch with our friend Jack Waterman, who had given me a lot of good advice when writing the book.

On the morning of the luncheon, a crisp October day, I had my usual attack of nerves before we set off for the station.

'Do you think I look all right? Do you think these really are the right shoes?'

'You look marvellous,' said Don. 'There's no need to flap, petal. Pretend it's an everyday thing and that they're going to be everyday women there.'

'But they're not!' I said. 'They're going to be Ladies, and Duchesses, and Dames, and all the top women . . .'

99

'Well, don't worry,' he said. 'They'll all be looking at Emma, anyway.'

At least he was right there.

We sat on the train going down, and I re-did my hair about three times until Don threatened to confiscate my comb.

'You look marvellous,' he said again, 'you really do. You must stop panicking.'

But I didn't stop panicking for a minute.

We arrived in London, took a taxi to the Savoy, and Don went off to meet Jack. 'Well, I hope you'll have as good a lunch as we do,' he said. 'We're having oysters!' Then he added more seriously, 'The best of luck, petal.'

It was not until Emma and I were going through the foyer, through the bustle of well-dressed women, with photographers' flash-bulbs going off every second, that, oddly, I somehow gained confidence. We're both a part of all this, I thought. Isn't it unbelievable!

A photographer came forward and took our picture, and we both stood trying to look elegant: I think Emma achieved it better than I did. We went into the reception and were introduced to a bewildering array of important women, and everyone seemed so pleased to see us, and made us so welcome. Then we took our seats in the enormous dining-room, with about six hundred women, and the noise from six hundred women, all talking, is indescribable. There were five speakers, and I was to speak after lunch. I very much wished I could have got it over beforehand.

During the tour promoting the book I had become used to TV cameras, but I began to think that TV cameras were far more friendly than six hundred women. I was absolutely terrified of making the speech, even though it was going to last only four minutes. Also, I had no idea what I was actually going to say—I never have until I get to my feet, and out it all comes— or at least it always had so far.

The sad thing is that, to this day, I cannot remember what we had for lunch. I knew that when we got back everyone would want to know what it was like having lunch at the Savoy, and I simply never remembered what we had to eat because I was so nervous. By contrast, Emma, whom I could feel down by my feet, was quite comfortable, head between her paws, and quite oblivious to the importance of everybody and everything.

At last came my turn to speak. I knew this because the toast-master came and placed an enormous double microphone in front of me. I stood up and hoped no one noticed that I was shaking. I glanced round six hundred expectant faces, and I started:

I'm so delighted that I've been asked to come and speak to you about loyalty. I feel more equipped than most people to be able to talk about that subject because Emma, of course, has been so loyal to me over so many years and now it's my opportunity to show loyalty to her by only going to places where she's welcome as well. I look back and think of the times she took me to work or to do the shopping. It didn't matter where I wanted to go, or when, or what mood she was in, she'd always take me. Well, unless it was raining . . .

They all laughed. Thank goodness, I thought, at least I've got them laughing. I felt Emma get up at my feet, turn round and flop down again with the long-suffering groan which always meant: 'Well, this isn't very comfortable, you know. I hope you're not going to be long.' She was lying across both my feet, and I was standing trying to balance and keep my mind on the speech at the same time. It was very awkward. I continued:

She got to know my home town, Nottingham, like the back of her paw. She'd always find the shops that we went to regularly, just by the name of them. And unfailingly, regardless of what I told Emma to do, she somehow did the right thing. We had a new shopping centre in Nottingham. They put the bus station in there as well so it meant that Emma and I had to go through it to catch our bus at night. The first time that we went in I was absolutely lost because, being a big shopping centre, it had no kerbs or roads to cross so I just couldn't tell where I was going. I just had to rely on Emma's judgement. I knew that we had to find steps to go upstairs. One of the girls at work had told me that. 'You walk quite a long way down,' she said, 'and there's a flight of steps to go into the new bus station.' We seemed to be going for a long time so I told Emma to wait and I stopped one of the passers-by I'd heard. 'Can you tell me where the steps up to the bus station are?' I asked. 'Oh yes, just a few yards along there.' 'Come on Emma, find the steps,' I said. She took me a bit further along and stopped. Then she backed off a few paces. I put one foot forward and felt a step in front of me. 'Good girl,' I told her, 'you've found the steps. Come on then, off we go.' Emma backed off again. 'Come on Emma, up the steps. We've got to go into the new bus station.' She just wouldn't move. I tried to persuade her. 'Come on, Emma, we'll be late.' I started to get a little bit annoyed with her. But she wouldn't have it. She turned left instead and swung me round with her and trotted along. She just wouldn't listen to my pleas about going up steps. Then she stopped again and I heard a familiar sound: a lift coming down. I gave up. I knew Emma's preference was always for lifts rather than steps, but it seemed unusual for for her to sidetrack my instructions.

We got into the lift, and got out at the next floor up. We were in the bus station and I heard the driver of our bus who always said 'Good evening—and how's Emma?' He was never interested in how *I* was. I told him that she had brought me up in the lift and wouldn't go up the steps that someone had told me were the quickest way. 'I'm not sur-prised,' he said. 'They've only done the bottom three. The rest of it's a big hole. Good job she didn't take you up there—that dog's got more sense than most people.'

They all applauded and I felt so pleased as I sat down and felt Emma's nose come and touch my hand and heard her tail swishing under the table. Afterwards I was astonished at the number of guests who came up and said, 'Oh you did so well'. And Emma had her fans as well. Scores of women came up specially to meet Emma, to pat her and say hello, and stroke her. She was *the* guest among the Women of the Year.

But the best tribute to her came from a man. During lun-cheon, a waiter had very kindly come up and asked me if Emma would like anything to eat. I thanked him and said that she would not have anything to eat, but she would very much like a drink. So he brought some water for her—in a silver champagne bucket!

Afterwards he said: 'Madam, you know I've served all sorts of celebrities, from royalty to film stars, but I don't think I've ever before had the pleasure of serving a dog—and, if I may say, every inch a celebrity, and a lovely one at that.'

Emma at the Savoy had certainly become a V.I.P. and, as time went on, it became evident that this was not to be her only big occasion.

CHAPTER NINE

TOURING WITH THE book gave me some insight into the life of a celebrity. It was worthwhile but wearing: we piled into the car for Newcastle one day, Harrogate the next, and finished the week in the West Country perhaps; Don organized everything down to the last scrap of Emma's food; Emma herself, conserving her energy, slept in her place on the back seat, and was always ready—like the star she had become—to make her appearance on cue and never to disappoint her public. I signed copies of the book in endless bookshops, but I think most of the readers who brought it open ready at the title page, particularly the children as they unfailingly bent down to stroke Emma's brown head, secretly wished that she herself could have put her pawprint on the book; they would, I am sure, have preferred that to my signature.

Hotel rooms, late nights, broadcasting and television studios, snatched meals, interviews, the miles rolling by: the year went along in a whirl, and always accompanied by the anxiety that it should not be too much for little Emma, who, after all, was entitled to enjoy her retirement and not to have it made a penance. There was also, of course, Kerensa to look after and, when at home, the cats and my small private cattery. I was thankful, then, that I had not expanded it to the ultimate limit of my ambitions.

The eccentricities of some of the visitors were quite enough to cope with; but, as if that were not enough, my own cats provided extra zest to a life the pattern of which I considered quite rich enough to be going on with. Particularly Ming.

Ming was and still is the leader of the felines in the family, and she holds a special council every morning in the cat room— the special room off the kitchen I designed and had built for the Siamese to sleep and have their meals in. I think the most infuriating thing is that I *know* when Ming is holding her council. In the most calculating way she teaches any newcomers to the family how to do essential things, like taking pieces of steak off the kitchen table or walking on window ledges; how to get on to the pelmets without being noticed; or the easiest way to cause a disturbance in the hall when dinner time is near and thereby hasten the food along. However, she has never yet managed to transmit to another cat her unrivalled cunning in helping to augment Emma's diet. She keeps that trick strictly for herself. She sneaks on to the stove or the kitchen surfaces out of Emma's reach to commandeer a tasty morsel and bat it down with her paw to her eager and ever-greedy chocolate-brown accomplice below.

One night when we had all returned fairly exhausted from one of our book-signing expeditions, Ming decided to try out her escape routine. She must be extremely intelligent because she plans her escapes and seizes the vital moment. She would have been a tremendous asset in Colditz. She waits until she knows I am in total chaos—Kerensa has emptied a box of tea-bags on the floor and Emma is trying to eat them, the potatoes are boiling over, the telephone is ringing and Don is late. That is the ideal situation for a Ming Escape. On this occasion I think Kerensa had opened the back door, Don had gone to put the car away, and I was trying to get together a scratch meal. When I turned round, no Ming. It was pitch black outside— another requisite Ming chooses very carefully. She never escapes in daylight. And she knows I can't see in the dark.

I grabbed the torch out of the kitchen cupboard and dashed outside. The torch wouldn't work. Why? Kerensa had taken the batteries out. Luckily (and a chink in the cleverness per-haps) Ming gives a Geronimo shriek of delight when she gets outside, and I located her by ear somewhere near the dustbins. Now our dustbin area was not at that moment a pretty sight. The dustbin men were due the next day, and the rubbish was piled up; in addition there were some wooden boxes—some-thing Don had had delivered for the surgery—lying about waiting to be taken away. Ming had scooted over the boxes and down the fence at the other side. I scooted after her and im-mediately put my foot into one of the wooden boxes because I couldn't see the piled-up rubbish. Then I couldn't get my foot out. I tried, and, as I did so, heard Ming shrieking off down the garden so I had to gallop after her with a wooden box on one foot. I made a grab for her and missed, and not until later could I see anything funny in the scene, with boxes crashing and cats screaming and me stamping about. I had to give in, retired to the kitchen to admit defeat until the morning and set about getting the wooden box off my foot. As I did so I am sure I heard the distant equivalent of a Siamese cat laugh.

As a result of this sort of misbehaviour I find I constantly have to Think Ming. When I open a window I judge the space to see if it is Ming-sized. If it is, I close it down a bit. The same with doors. Whenever doors are opened or closed I have to Think Ming. It doesn't matter where there is a hole or gap, Ming will find it. In the bungalow where we used to live, the bathroom and the kitchen backed on to each other so that all the water system and pipes and drainage were together. So, from the bathroom (if you were a cat, that is) you could proceed through the linen cupboard, underneath the bath panelling, underneath the sink cupboard, and would emerge by the fridge in the kitchen. This was quite an accomplishment, and Ming used it to great advantage. If I shut her out of the living-room or the kitchen, she could always try the bathroom for size. This Houdini trick always worked. She appeared from nowhere in the kitchen to steal whatever food had foolishly been left out— or, if she was not particularly hungry, pass it on to Emma.

Ming just cannot understand human beings not liking cats. She will not accept the fact at all. She believes that everyone is an ardent worshipper of the Siamese breed. Not everyone is, of course, but at least she has one important unwavering ally to keep up her morale, and that is Emma.

So it can be seen that even if I only had Ming there would be quite enough to keep me occupied, in addition to touring with the book and other activities. Among the other activities I tried to keep going (voluntarily, that is) was showing my Siamese. This had all started with Ohpas, my Red Point, who died some years ago. When a friend came round and said how beautiful he was, I just could not resist showing him to see if we were not all biased. But apparently we were not. He won a lot of prizes, and that got me hooked on to cat shows like a drug.

The extra bonus to this was, for me, making good friends. When I started showing cats (and Don helped with a great deal of the preparation and grooming) I could not see, and I found I had never before met such a set of people who would take me as I was and treat me like another human being. But I must admit, when I look at the show world as a whole, I realize how totally different it is, and appreciate that someone going to a cat show for the first time might find it very odd.

Each cat is penned with his or her own white blanket, and a white feeding bowl. Every cat must have identical equipment, and the owners are not allowed into the hall while the cats are being judged: so everything is completely fair. But the sort of conversation that goes on would really strike someone not used to cat shows as rather strange. At lunch-time we all pile back into the hall after the judging to look hopefully for those big rosettes that mean First. And that, these days, is very nice for me: to be able to see the rosettes. I never could when I started showing. I would get a friend to lead me up to the pen where my cat was and I would feel round in the hope of a rosette. I would say, 'Don't tell me. Don't tell me if there's anything on the pen. Let me feel for it.'

These days I can go and look—and, of course, get the disappointment that much sooner if there is no rosette. Yet, although we have had our disappointments, the hall and living-room bear witness to the success of the cats, for there are scores of rosettes all round the walls from all over the country. But one rosette, a green and gold one, has pride of place, and it is the only one that was not earned by one of the Siamese. It is Emma's rosette, and every time I see it I still get a glow of tremendous pride for her. It is a Cruft's rosette earned as a Personality Dog of the Year in 1978, and you cannot be anything other than a canine V.I.P. to gain this award, the highlight of the show on its final day.

When the invitation to take part arrived from Cruft's I was thrilled beyond belief. But as the day approached I became obsessed with the idea that Emma had to do herself justice in front of the crowds—and all the other dogs, of course, champions included. It was her due, I thought, that she would be not only a personality dog, but *the* star of the parade.

'What can I do to make her look really nice?' I asked Don.
'She always looks nice,' he said.

'Do you think she ought to have a bath?'

'Don't mention that word,' he said quickly. But not quickly enough. Emma's ears had twitched at an unpopular sound and she took herself off into the kitchen with a very quizzical expression on her face.

'Oh, I forgot!' I said. 'Well, what I'll do is to pretend that *I'm* going to have a bath. I'll go upstairs and start getting all my clothes into the bathroom like I always do, and run the water and sing.'

'That'll put her off,' he said with a grin.

'No, no, you know what I mean—make her think it's me that's getting into the bath, not her. She always comes and sits in the bathroom with me.'

'I bet it doesn't work,' he said.

'Oh, it will if I really pretend, really make it convincing,' I said. 'I'll take my bubble bath in and make sure she sees me do it.'

'I bet it doesn't work,' Don repeated unhelpfully.

I went off upstairs, ran the water and started to sing, throwing perfume about, gathering clothes into the bathroom and hiding the towels for Emma underneath them. Normally, by the time the taps are running Emma is upstairs, curled up on the bathroom floor. But this time there was no sign of her.

'Is she still down there?' I called to Don.

'Yes, in the kitchen, by the back door,' he shouted.

'Oh dear. Do you think she knows?'

'I'm sure she does. You'll never get her up there.'

'Well, we can't carry her upstairs, she's too heavy. See if you can get her to come up. Try and get her into the hall.' At the same time I started calling her. Don, I could hear, was also calling. 'Come on Emma, into the hall, there's a good girl.'

But nothing happened. Emma remained a chocolate-brown immovable object by the back door, gazing up with an expression which stated very plainly: 'I know what you want to do. And you can keep on wanting.'

I came downstairs. 'What are we going to do about it?'

Sheila, Emma, Kerensa, summer 1979

Kerensa and Emma

(*from left*) Bracken,
Buttons and Emma

Colonel and Mrs Clay with Emma's mother

Bracken with his dumb-bell

'I've no idea. She knows you want to give her a bath, and she knows you're pretending.'

Then I spotted the box of chocolate drops with added vitamins that Emma loved and which she used to get as rewards. I picked it off the shelf. 'I wonder,' I said, 'if greed will get the better of her hatred of baths?'

Emma saw me doing this, and immediately became alert and anxious all at the same time. Her nose twitched. I offered her a chocolate drop. She got up and came towards me and took it, munching thoughtfully and giving a small wag of the tail. I retreated into the hall.

'Come on, Emma, another chocolate drop.'

I could see the thinks-balloon: 'What's this? *Another* chocolate drop. Well . . . why not? What does it matter if there *is* a catch?'

She took it. I ventured to the stairs. Emma stood watching me a little more warily. But she couldn't resist, and even though it ended up with me putting a chocolate drop on every other step, she was finally manoeuvred into the bathroom.

'I've got her,' I called down to Don, 'It's OK.'

I lifted her into the bath. Poor Emma. She stood there looking so dejected and woeful, but also resigned. 'I knew all along this is what you wanted!' she seemed to be saying.

'I'm sorry Emma,' I said. 'I really am sorry. But you're going to Cruft's, you know, and it's the biggest dog show in the world, and you're going to be best dog there and the best there's ever been.'

Perhaps it didn't make up for having a bath, but when she was finally dried down and brushed she really did look beautiful.

On the following day Don, Emma and I went down to London on the train. When we go by train we have to find a compartment with a carpet on the floor because Emma doesn't like plain boards. After all, she is getting on in years, and she does deserve her comforts. Once on the carpet, with the train pulling out of Nottingham Midland, she put her head between her paws and went to sleep.

'I wonder what she'll think of all the dogs?' Don said. 'She'll never have seen so many dogs together.'

'No,' I said, patting her. 'But what will all the other dogs think of Emma? They ought to realize she's somebody special. After all, she's not just a show dog. She's a Personality Dog.' And I leaned down and gave another stroke to the sleeping, dreaming form at my feet.

When we got to Olympia we were amazed at the queues of people waiting to get in. As we got into the bustle and noise inside I turned to Don and said: 'There's a sort of smell in the air.'

'You mean dogs,' he said.

'No, no. A smell of stardom and sawdust.'

'Emma's not like that,' Don said. 'She takes everything in her stride. She's never changed since the book came out.'

'Oh, do you mean I have?' I said.

'No, of course not. But you know what I mean. It doesn't matter what Emma does or where she goes, she's always the same Emma, isn't she? Even if she is picked as Personality Dog of the Year.'

Suddenly I felt a tug on the lead. Emma had spotted a Weimerana.

'No, that's not Zelda,' I told her. Then she was distracted by a bull mastiff on the other side. 'She doesn't know where to go first, does she?'

She put her nose into the air, smelling in every direction. It was so exciting for her. Sniff, sniff, sniff—what a wonderful place to be!

We all gathered in a little room off the main hall, all the owners and dogs that had been picked to appear in the Personality Parade. The old English bulldog was there, the Labradors from the Drug Squad, the police Alsatians—even K9 was there, not a real dog at all, but the little mechanical robot from the *Dr Who* programme on TV. I wondered what Emma would make of him when she saw him.

We were then briefed for the Personality Parade, and I was amazed at how much effort and organization had gone into this one event. The Cruft's man responsible gathered us round a blackboard. On it he had drawn the ring and I saw that there were various numbers round a carpet, a red carpet this would be, stretching right across the ring. Everyone had a number, he told us, and we would all be called in by number when our time came. We were expected to walk into the ring, up the red carpet and stop in the middle as the commentator gave all the details of why our dogs had been picked for Personality Dog of that year.

'There'll be a big crowd out there,' he said, 'twenty-five thousand, and they'll all be interested in what your dog does, so you must stop in the middle of the ring while we commentate and everyone can get a good look at your dog.'

Our number was twenty. When he got to that he said: 'They'll be interested to know why Emma is a Personality Dog. We normally have a guide-dog in, but then Emma has not only been a guide-dog, she's also had a book written about her. That makes her special.'

Later on in the afternoon we gathered by the ring for the big moment. Don stood with Emma and me.

'I wish you could come in there with us,' I told him.

'Not likely,' he said, 'with all those lights and cameras and people watching. No, you and Emma go. You'll be all right when you get there. You're used to this sort of thing.'

'Not *this* sort of thing,' I said apprehensively. But Emma didn't seem to mind. She wagged her tail and looked up. 'Yes,' I said, 'it *is* something special isn't it Emma? This is really your show.'

'It's only what she deserves,' said Don, and added, 'Doesn't she look marvellous after her bath? Stand up to any of these champions!'

Then we were given our rosette. Each dog that appeared in the Personality Parade got a big rosette. I gripped it tight as I waited for the event to start. There was a fanfare of trumpets over the loudspeakers, and the announcer came on.

'Number One,' he called. He went through a description of each dog and what it had done throughout the year. I was so nervous I had to listen really hard for our number. At last it came.

'Number Twenty,' he called, 'Emma.' I was pushed into the ring by one of the organizers. 'In you go,' he said.

Emma and I walked into the floodlights to huge applause and cheering. As we walked down the red carpet I could hear the commentator reading passages out of the book, telling stories of when Emma was a guide-dog, how clever she was, and how she found me a phone-box when my usual one had broken down. And suddenly there was the magic again, the something that we had lost after I could see. I could feel the tension on the lead as it used to be on the harness as Emma walked proudly to the centre of the ring. Without me telling her she just stopped and sat down and faced the commentator and looked round at the mass of faces: thousands and thousands of people all applauding and cheering her. It was incredible, and such an emotional moment. I wanted to applaud with them and shout and laugh because none of this was for me, it was all for little Emma.

Then we had to walk off down the red carpet to our allotted number which was painted on the floor. I wished I could have watched it all from a spectator's point of view—each dog coming in, stopping, going off to take their position so that finally the ring contained a huge circle of Personality Dogs.

Emma, true to form, lay down and went to sleep: that is, until she heard K9, the last 'dog' in the parade coming in at the opposite side of the ring. His hum and clicking noise woke her. She sat up, ears forward, and tested the air. A strange sort of smell was obviously coming from that thing. He got closer, and Emma started to back off from the red carpet. As K9 trundled and whirred past with his electrical lead she looked up at me as if to say: 'Well, I thought this was a dog show. What's that thing doing in here, then?'

After K9 had taken up his position, Emma lay down again and went back to sleep. She stayed asleep, quite oblivious, until the finale when we were all paraded again back up the red carpet and out of the ring.

And that red carpet, I thought, as we passed from it and out of the arclights, was the right setting for Emma, for ever. It had been her greatest day, and as I pinned the great green and gold rosette over our fireplace in the living-room later that evening, and Emma was stretched in front of the fire as if nothing had happened, I also thought: At last she has had her recognition, her due, and her rightful accolade. Good girl Emma!

CHAPTER TEN

BEING A Personality Dog of the Year, appearing on television chat shows, and being a star at bookshops all over the country were the highlights of Emma's new career. But the admiration at these events was more than equalled by fans calling on her personally, and by an astonishing postbag. Scores of letters began to arrive as a result of the book. Some, mostly from children, were addressed direct to Emma. These I always read aloud, which may sound eccentric, but I felt it logical and only right to pass on the praise to the right quarter when they said how marvellous Emma was, how clever she was to find that telephone-box on her own and so on. Emma knows when approving things are being said about her and always sat beside me on the settee when her fan mail arrived. Invariably her response was one of those old-fashioned looks meaning: 'Well, what do they expect? I was a guide-dog, after all.' And I had to smile. Sometimes at moments like that she reminded me of a rather languid Hollywood screen goddess reclining while her secretary dealt out the adulation from the correspondence: 'OK Beulah, send 'em a photograph.' And, of course, if a photograph had been requested, it was me that had to sign it and send it off. By the third or fourth letter, however, Emma had usually had enough flattery for one day, and I would hear the unmistakable sound of her sliding down the leather back of the settee, and a slight satisfied sigh before she put her head between her paws and went to sleep.

There was one sad aspect of the letters, nevertheless, because invariably they would ask, 'Is Emma still alive? How is she?' It was fine then, and still is, being able to write back and say, 'She's full of beans.' But I know that one day I shall not be able to do that; it's going to be heartbreaking to read letters with those questions. One day perhaps I shall not be able to reply at all. I don't know. I try not to think about it, but all the time

I am conscious of how sad it is that animals do not live as long as human beings.

The letters I liked best of all were the ones in which the writer said that the book had not simply entertained them, but helped them as well. I particularly liked one from a primary school teacher who said that every morning at assembly she read out a passage from *Emma and I* and *never* had she known the children so quiet.

More seriously, I was most moved when a woman who had undergone a really serious operation wrote to me: '. . . when I came round from the operation I thought, I'm not going to be miserable. But I can't get out of bed. What shall I do? Then I thought about your book, so I looked out of the window and counted all the different colours of all the leaves on the trees, and that kept me occupied until I could get up and out of bed.' I was so moved by that, someone who had gone through the most traumatic experience being helped through it by what I had written. It made me happy, too, because other people had told me how different I had made their lives by telling them what it was like to see for the first time, and how they themselves now saw things with more appreciation. Whenever people told me this I always thought of the time I was coming back from London on the train one evening. It had been a brilliant summer day, and as the train sped north to Nottingham there was the most incredible sunset: great rays of red and gold through banks of slate-blue cloud as we reached the Trent, with dazzling reflections in the water as if somehow the sun were submerged in the river like a great molten blood orange.

There were five others in the compartment with me, all businessmen. Three were asleep, one was doing a crossword, and the other was hidden by his *Financial Times*. I wanted to get on my seat and shout at them: 'Look! Wake up! Can't you see what's happening? Isn't it marvellous! Why don't you use your eyes for something important? Something wonderful that will never ever happen again exactly as it is now!' But I just sat there, and the eyes of those asleep remained closed, while the man doing the crossword gazed up momentarily but sightlessly as he pondered a clue and the other man stayed hidden behind

his paper, and by then we were slowing up through the Nottingham shunting yards and the sun finally vanished behind the
great black warehouse which housed the British Waterways, a
minute before drawing into Midland Station.

So many people don't really see what is going on around
them. They take their gift of sight so much for granted. They
look at grass and never think, that's wonderful grass. If it
changed colour overnight they would probably never notice.
I was glad the people had written to me and said that my
description of getting sight had given them new eyes as well.

Apart from the letters there were innumerable callers. Particularly on Sundays: children on the doorstep, old ladies,
entire families saying, 'We're sorry to bother you, but we've
read your book. Could we see Emma do you think?' At least
Emma didn't bark automatically every time the doorbell went.
When we first moved to the surgery the doorbell sounded like
the telephone back at the bungalow, and the telephone either
bleeped on a direct line, or buzzed when a call was routed from
the surgery. At first, for good measure, Emma barked at all
three. But within a fortnight she had learnt the differences. Who
says you can't teach an old dog new tricks?

But the publication of *Emma and I* was having another effect.
We were now getting cheques for royalties and foreign rights,
and each one brought a little more hope that one day, very
much in the future but one day nevertheless, we might realize
our ambition of buying our own boarding cattery and kennels.
At first I had intended simply to buy a commercial cattery as
a going concern and to develop the kennels later—although had
it not been for Emma the priorities would have been reversed.
I didn't think it would have been fair on Emma to have other
dogs around. When Emma was out in the park, or nosing her
way over the fields above our house where Don particularly
liked to take her, she loved it when she met other dogs. But if
we had friends in who brought a dog with them, then Emma
went all peculiar. The expression on her face said: 'What's this!
Another dog in *my* house!' She didn't *do* anything, nor make
any sign of aggression; she was even polite to them, in a distant
sort of way, but she would not play with them however much
they woofed around her and lay doggo pleading: 'Oh do come

and play.' Emma always remained aloof, and the look on her face also meant when she glanced up at us: 'I don't mind whether you have babies, or cats, or as many people as you like—but, please, not other dogs in here. Please.' So that is why, although the desire to run a kennels of my own dated back to the years when I was a girl, unable to see, getting weekend jobs at local dog establishments round Nottingham, I originally gave a greater priority to buying a commercial cattery.

So for a long time the idea of, ultimately, owning kennels was something even more remote than the cattery—and of course I had built only a private little cattery at the back of the house for the offspring of my own cats. But gradually Don and I came round to the view that eventually, when we had the money, Emma would probably not mind if she remained the centre of attention in the house and there were dogs boarded in whatever new establishment we could buy. At the same time it never entered my head—or Don's for that matter—to have another dog in the house. We both worshipped Emma, and any permanent intrusion would seem such an affront to her. Or so we thought.

But one evening Don was sitting watching television and I was reading my favourite part of the local newspaper—*not* the news columns which are invariably miserable and depressing, but the 'For Sale' section. I lapped up every detail of 'Garden Sheds £20 o.n.o.' or 'Ford Cortina. As new', items that did not remotely concern me in my day to day existence, but which on the closely-printed page somehow acquired a magical attraction that compelled me to read about them. I got to the 'Dogs' column. I always read the 'Dogs' column, not particularly because I wanted another dog, but I was very interested to know about the dogs for sale, what breed they were and how much owners were charging. Suddenly something seemed to leap out of the page towards me. It was something I had never seen advertised before. I couldn't believe it. 'Chocolate-coloured Labrador,' it said. 'One year old.' I read it again. Sure enough, my eyes had not deceived me. 'Chocolate-coloured Labrador.' How about that? I thought. I suppose I had really come to think that Emma was the only chocolate-coloured Labrador in the whole world. They were so unusual that I had never seen another, let alone read an ad. for one, and I was resigned to people coming up to me and saying, 'Isn't she lovely! What breed is she?'

'Don,' I said, 'read that advert.' I thrust the paper under his nose.

'Mm, what advert?' he said, not taking his eyes off the screen.

'Look, this advert. Read it. What does it say?'

He took the paper from me and looked rather blankly at the page of ads.

'What do you mean, "What does it say"? Which one?'

I pointed it out.

'Read it to me,' I said.

He was still rather puzzled, but looked intently at the page.

'Chocolate-coloured Labrador . . .' he began, but by the time he had got that far he was alive with interest and astonishment. 'One year old.'

He handed the paper back to me.

'Incredible,' he said.

'Yes isn't it?' There was a pause, and in the silence I think our two minds were racing along the same lines. But it was Don who beat me to expressing what we were thinking:

'I wonder what she looks like?' he said.

'Yes, so do I.' I suppose it never occurred to either of us, having lived with Emma so long, that 'she' might possibly have been 'he'. There was a further pause.

'Do you think it's worth ringing them?' I said.

'Well,' said Don, a little uncertain, 'you could ask them what she's like.'

'Mm. I'm really intrigued. I just wonder how like Emma she is.'

'I wonder,' said Don. 'You can't do any harm just giving them a ring.'

I picked up the phone. Then, when halfway through dialling the number given in the paper, a thought struck me. I put the phone down again.

'What's the matter?' said Don.

'I've just thought. What do I say? It sounds a bit daft, really . . . "Hello Mrs Whatever, I've rung about your chocolate-coloured Labrador . . . I don't want to make an offer for her, but I just want to know what she's like because we've got one as well . . ." She'll think we're barmy.'

Don burst out laughing.

'Go on,' he said, 'ring up and ask. They won't mind. We could fix up to go and see her.' And he added: 'You never know, we might like her.'

'Oh,' I said, 'I don't know about that.' It somehow seemed terribly disloyal, what we were doing. Emma was curled up, all oblivious, asleep in her usual place on the settee, dreaming with an occasional little sound and a twitch of her forepaw. I looked at her. There was really only one chocolate-coloured Labrador in the world.

'I don't know,' I said again, and gave a sigh. 'I don't think Emma would like it. And I think it would be a bit unfair to go along and see the dog without any intention of buying.'

Don thought for a moment. Finally he said: 'Well, don't you think Emma likes other dogs?'

'Oh, of course she does. But whether she would like another one living here's a different thing.'

Somehow, without discussing it, we seemed to have got to the possibility that we might—just *might*—consider buying the dog, and that seemed even more underhand. I put the idea out of my head.

'Well,' said Don, 'they won't mind you ringing up to inquire. Ring them up and ask what kind of a price they're thinking of, and then see where we go from there.'

'All right,' I said. It was curiosity really that got the better of me. I so much wanted to see this other chocolate-coloured Labrador. But I was quite determined that we would not buy her.

I picked up the phone again. A woman answered. Yes, the voice said, she (it *was* a 'she') was still for sale. 'Why do you want to sell her?' I asked. 'I'm afraid I've got too many dogs,' was the answer, 'and I've just had another litter of ten. They all need hand-feeding and I haven't time to cope with the others properly so I thought the best thing was to try and find them good homes.'

'I understand. I wonder would it be possible for us to come

and have a look? I'm not sure whether we want another dog, and I'd really quite like to bring our dog to see her.'

This all came out with a bit of a rush, and judging by the silence at the other end, I felt the woman was thinking I was slightly deranged.

But, rather uncertainly, she agreed and we arranged to go the following day. I put the phone down. Don was back watching his programme and I didn't say anything to him. Thoughts raced through my head. I sat on the settee beside Emma. Another dog. Another chocolate-coloured Labrador. Emma shifted in her sleep. I wonder if she'll look at all like Emma? I wonder if she has the same sort of temperament? No, not possibly. Never another like Emma. What would Emma think if we brought another dog home? Like bringing Kerensa home ... another child, another baby. Emma certainly had not been too keen on Kerensa to begin with, but then had accepted her as a person. Another dog would be worse. Or would it be better? I decided not to worry about it. We would just go and see her.

So the next day, Don, Emma and I, and, of course, Kerensa, set out to have a look at this rarity, another chocolate-coloured Labrador. When the breeder answered the door and saw Emma I think she had a shock.

'Oh, I had no idea you'd got a chocolate Labrador already...'

'Yes, but we've never seen another, and we would very much like to see yours ... I don't know whether we want to buy another dog.' (I felt I had to be quite honest.) 'It all depends on Emma, and what she thinks ...'

The breeder was sympathetic. She smiled.

'I understand. Do come in.'

'Does she like other dogs?' I asked.

'Yes, she loves other dogs.'

'And what about children?'

'Yes, she likes children. In fact, altogether, she's really a very friendly dog ... anyway sit down and I'll go and fetch her.'

We all sat down. I was feeling apprehensive, I don't know why. What would this dog be like? Was I going to be disappointed? What did I expect? To be honest I hardly knew.

But before I had more than a few seconds to think, the door opened and in bounded a shiny, young, tail-wagging chocolate Labrador. In an instant my mind went back years: to the Guide-Dog Training Centre at Leamington Spa, sitting on the edge of my bed, the door open, waiting. My eyes had not seen anything, but my mind had preserved every detail of that moment as clearly as if it had happened only a second before. Sitting, waiting, then hearing footsteps approaching down the corridor outside, and hearing an even more magic sound keeping pace with them . . . the click and unmistakable patter of paws . . .

Then I heard the trainer's voice: 'Here we are, Sheila . . . here's your dog. She's called Emma, and she's a chocolate-coloured Labrador . . .'

And I had heard a tail swishing the air and the trainer leaving, closing the door behind him. 'Emma,' I had called, and immediately had been aware of a bounding in the room and being nearly bowled off the bed, and then being licked all over. 'Hello, Emma,' I had said, 'hello.' And, as I felt a cold nose pushing into my hands, I remember thinking that I couldn't believe it. It was a dream. This was Emma, and she liked me, and I had felt like dancing round the room.

And now, in this room, I could see something of what it must have been like. And yet at the same time I knew it was just an approximation, because the moment that Emma came into my life was unique and nothing would ever match it.

However, in bounded Buttons, full of glee, full of excitement, vigour and life, leaping immediately up to Emma and making a big fuss of her before she even noticed that Emma belonged to other human beings. When she had got over the excitement of meeting Emma, she came over to us, tail going sixty to the dozen, brown nose glistening, ears bouncing up and down, coat so glossy and with all those different shades of colours that Emma also had. I took her in at a glance and knew immediately that she was not completely like Emma. She was different: she was herself; yet alike also, merely because of the fact she was chocolate-coloured. I have to be honest and say that from the moment she came in, I fell in love with Buttons and it did not diminish one speck my love for Emma.

'Can I take them into the garden?' I asked. 'I want to see if she will play with Emma, and if Emma will want to play with her.'

'Yes, of course.'

Emma was then thirteen years old and obviously she had begun to slow down, but it was not until we met Buttons that I realized how much. It is strange how you grow old with your dog, and you expect them to do only what an older dog will do. Emma was beginning to plod a little along the pavements, to make her strolls across the park more leisurely, and to stop and sniff a little more before moving on to the next bush or tree.

In the garden we let both the dogs off the lead. Buttons danced about and immediately did the usual Labrador thing: bottom and tail in the air, nose and front paws along the ground, tail gently wagging, making those little snorting and snuffling noises, the appeal of all these friendliest of all creatures: 'Come and play with me. Oh do come and play.'

Emma's response was to behave a little like a shocked Victorian lady who has had an improper suggestion made to her on a park bench, her expression almost shrouded in lace frills and disapproval: 'If you think I'm simply an ordinary dog, you're very, very much mistaken.'

Then, all at once, the disdain and haughtiness vanished. She changed utterly. Instincts and long-forgotten memories stirred. It was as if, in a second, she shed years and years. She dashed over to Buttons and then they took off, chasing round and round, together, in among the flower beds, skidding over the lawn, disappearing round a far hedge and reappearing time and time again, until they both came to a stop in front of us and, as Labradors do, suddenly flumped themselves down, tongues out, panting, exhausted and happy.

Don and I looked at each other.

'What do you think?' Don said.

'I think she's beautiful.'

'Well . . .?'

'Well . . . Emma likes her . . . it's obvious . . .'

Still neither of us could take the decision, or rather speak the decision that each of us had mentally made.

'Do you think Emma would really like her to play with permanently?'

'I don't know,' said Don, stroking them both. 'What do you think Buttons? Would you like to come and live with Emma?' And to Emma: 'What do you think about it, Emma?'

They both panted and wagged their tails, beating them on the grass in unison. It was as good an answer as we would ever get from them.

I took from my bag an extra lead I had brought—almost unconsciously, thinking: Just in case.

'Come on Buttons,' I said, 'come on Emma.' We paid for Buttons there and then. The breeder was delighted. And so were we. All of us. Kerensa kept saying, 'Two Emmas.'

I tried to explain that there were not really two Emmas, but it was difficult for her to get her tongue round the name Buttons. 'Bundle,' she said valiantly, and then looked up at me and persisted, 'Mummy, look—two Emmas.' I had to give in.

In the car going back Buttons showed that she was really well behaved. She sat on the back seat with Emma, and with Kerensa in between them, not at all perturbed that strangers had come and taken her away from what had been her home for a whole year, not at all anxious about travelling in a car.

We drove home. I was very happy. But a thought occurred to me as we got nearer.

'I wonder what Emma will think when we all go into the house together.'

Don kept his eyes on the road, and I was a bit surprised by his reaction because he is the least hard-hearted of men.

'She'll have to go back,' he said, drawing up to some traffic lights and turning to look at me as he put the hand brake on. 'She'll have to go back if Emma doesn't like it. Emma comes first, whatever happens.'

Then we were off again and nearing the drive to the house.

But I need not have worried. We all piled out and opened the front door, and Kerensa and the dogs all dashed in together, leaving Don and me on the doorstep just as if that is what had always happened.

Both Buttons and Emma rushed through the house and stood wagging their tails in the kitchen, waiting to go through into the garden. We let them out and that is all we saw of them until that strange Labrador alarm clock worked. They came in, shaking themselves and fussing round together precisely half an hour before feeding-time: Emma's old feeding-time that is. I set about putting the food out for them both, and when I put the bowls down together I knew that we had not made a mistake, or been disloyal, or done anything that was not for the best. There they stood together, two chocolate-brown shapes together, noses into the bowls. There was no jealousy from Emma or animosity from Buttons, and above all there was no sense that Emma had been displaced.

After their dinner, which had involved much sliding of bowls across the kitchen floor, Emma came into the living-room, and jumped up on to her usual place on the settee. Buttons sat herself on the floor and looked up longingly.

'No,' I said to her, 'that's Emma's place. I'm sorry, but Emma does get the best place and you'll have to sit on the floor.' So she sat there obediently, just as later, when we got a basket for her, she would always turn round when Emma went up on the settee and make for the kitchen and her basket.

Never once did Buttons attempt to get on the settee and never once did she attempt to push Emma out, and gradually I began to realize one important thing: however young and big and vigorous Buttons was compared with Emma who was small and getting on in years, Emma was boss. There was no question about it. No one could cross Emma, and least of all her new-found young friend Buttons.

There were times when Emma didn't want to play. Buttons would bound up with a rubber bone and push it at Emma's nose, and Emma would back off, shake herself, pretend Buttons wasn't there and walk away. Buttons knew. She decided it was always better not to push her point and, rather than follow Emma, she would go off into the garden and play on her own.

In the days that followed the advent of Buttons into the house both Don and I noticed a quite significant change in Emma, and not the sort of change that in our wildest dreams we could have anticipated. Emma's walks became romps, eager dashings from tree to tree instead of sedate perambulations with frequent stops for interesting sniffs. If Buttons and Emma were out together and they saw another dog, they both had to run and investigate; whereas before, Emma would have been interested but would have taken things in much slower time. Now it was important that they both showed themselves to be vigorous, honest, full-to-the-brim-with-living Labradors. I saw, physically and mentally, the years drop away from Emma. It was incredible and wonderful. Suddenly, with the company of Buttons, it was if she had been re-born, and, not long after, thankful as we were for that alone, we were to bless doubly the day that we had taken a new chocolate-brown shape into our midst.

CHAPTER ELEVEN

SOON AFTER BUTTONS had arrived on the scene—bounced would be a better word—I was due to go to the United States in connection with the publication of *Emma and I* over there. This had been worrying me for a variety of reasons. In the first place, the publishers had obviously hoped I would be able to take Emma with me and she would then have added to her prestige on the other side of the Atlantic personally. The trouble with that idea was, lovely as it would have been for Emma to take Broadway and Fifth Avenue by storm, we could not have got her back into this country without a six-month sentence in quarantine kennels. In other words, it was unthinkable that she should go to America.

But that, in turn, brought another problem: for twelve years Emma and I had never been separated, apart from the short intervals when I had gone into hospital for my eye operation and when Kerensa was born. But going to the United States without her was different again. I felt terrible at the thought. It seemed like abandoning her. Quite apart from that, since Emma was such a dominant attraction of the book, I didn't see why the publishers wanted to bother with just me going. Emma and I were such a team, and this seemed like going to play an away fixture with more than half the team on the injured list.

I really didn't want to go at all, but eventually I agreed with the greatest reluctance. My mother would come in to look after Kerensa. This may seem heartless but I had, strangely, less anxiety about leaving her than Emma. Kerensa was used to my mother and got on with her, as did Emma; but whereas I knew Kerensa would not lose sleep over me not being there, I was so afraid Emma might think it strange and might pine when she realized I had gone for more than twenty-four hours.

But as the day for our departure approached, I began to

realize that Emma would not necessarily lie on the hearth-rug moping. There she was, day after day, romping about with Buttons—and, far from being a staid old lady, behaving like a puppy herself. My misgivings and concern on her behalf evaporated. I knew Emma would be well occupied, and certainly distracted from wondering and worrying over where I had gone. If for no other reason, I was so glad we had taken the decision that had led to Buttons joining the family, and I blessed my habit of looking at the small ads in the *Nottingham Evening Post*.

There was, however, one remaining anxiety that was looming ever larger. I had never flown before, and the nearer the day for departure came, the more I did not want to change this blissful state of ignorance. I was, in truth, quite scared of the idea. There seemed no reason to me why aeroplanes should be able to defy gravity. Whenever I saw them, I always thought of the conjurer who announced, 'My next trick is impossible.' It didn't stand to reason—not my reason anyway—that aeroplanes should be able to move through the air without somehow being controlled by wires from the ground.

Perhaps one reason for my fear of flying was that when I was blind I was never able to visualize aeroplanes. I knew they were there because I could hear them, but I had no idea whatsoever what they looked like. I had no idea what birds looked like either. I knew, again, they were there because I could hear their lovely songs—quite unlike the terrible whining and roaring of aircraft—but I had simply no mental image of what they might be like. The difference was (and this may well be related to the difference of noise, and the difference between natural and unnatural things) that I quite liked the *idea* of birds but was rather disturbed by the idea of aircraft.

When I had got my sight back I saw aircraft and birds; and whereas before it had seemed beyond reason that anything could fly in the air, now seeing was believing. I remember calling Don out one day to show him a bird in a tree. He had wondered what I was on about. But it had seemed magical to me to see it in the branches of a tree where I had never imagined anything, and then to see it fly off. In the same way I was quite surprised when I actually saw an aeroplane, but it had not lessened my instinctive distrust of them. And it had not helped one night when we were coming back from doing an appearance for the book in Oxfordshire and I had seen great flashing lights in the sky getting nearer the road we were driving on. I had read about U.F.O.s, and thought this is it! I made Don stop the car and we parked by the road and watched, with a great golden moon making the scene even more strange. 'Don,' I said, 'is that a U.F.O.?' He had burst out laughing. 'No,' he said, 'it's an aircraft coming in with its landing lights on!' I felt rather silly, but it did not help to endear me to aircraft.

When the day came to go, my fears had transmitted themselves to Don, who, as always, tried to put my mind at rest. So did Don's partner in the practice, John Goodliffe, who had agreed to come along with us to see to and smooth out all the bits of organization which would be needed from day to day in America.

Unknown to them, however, I had that morning done something which helped to comfort me even more than all their kind words. Coming downstairs (avoiding Don who was rushing about with suitcases and little bits of paper with instructions for my mother), I had seen Emma's lead on the hall stand. A sudden inexplicable impulse had made me touch it. Then I had thought: Why not? Why not take it with me? This is Emma's special lead, but there are others if she and Buttons are taken for a walk while we're away. I lifted it quietly off the hook—so quietly that Emma's ears would not detect the usually promising clink of the metal clip—and put it in my handbag. I felt so relieved in a curious way. I felt that now I had something that physically bound me to Emma and it gave me confidence and a quite extraordinary sense that some of her marvellous presence would be with me.

So things were a little easier as we drove off at last. Kerensa was waving from my mother's arms on the front doorstep and Emma, having tried to get in the back of the car as usual, resignedly went off with Buttons. My final backward glance at her was not reciprocated: by then she was quite happily rolling on the lawn beyond the rose bushes with her young friend.

As we got nearer to London—we were making for Heathrow

Airport—I suddenly felt very thirsty. Whether this was another sign of apprehension I am not sure, but I said, 'Why don't we stop for a drink?'

John sounded dubious. 'I think we ought to get on,' he said. But Don agreed with me so we stopped at the next pub, which had a lovely garden, and sat outside in the late summer sunshine. I would cheerfully have sat there all afternoon and missed the plane, because as I sipped my tomato juice I kept thinking of the flight ahead and, when not dwelling on that prospect, I would be thinking of Kerensa, or, opening my bag for a cigarette, would see the lead and wonder what Emma was doing. What made things worse was that no sooner had we sat at the table than a big, handsome yellow Labrador dashed out of the pub and lolloped straight across to us. He was full of bright-eyed greetings, and tail waggings, and made me feel traitorous and terrible all over again.

But a thousand more anxieties later, including passport control and being searched for bombs, we were at last waiting to get on the aircraft. It was a Jumbo, and never in my life had I seen anything so big. We got to the steps. Don went first, then John. 'These are not steps into an aircraft,' I told myself. 'You are just going up into a room.' I closed my mind to the fact that the steps, which shook uncertainly as we went up them, led into an aeroplane. There was perspiration on my palms and I could feel my heart thumping. Once on board I sat sort of transfixed, in the middle seat between Don and John, and watched everyone else stowing hand baggage and air hostesses endlessly smiling toothpaste smiles, and, with a sinking feeling, heard the thump of the doors being closed and felt already removed from the world I knew. I wanted so much to put my hand down by the seat and feel an affectionate cold nose. But there was none, and I hoped telepathy did not work over the hundred-odd miles back to Emma in Nottingham, transmitting my fear to her.

The take-off was a rumbling, thumping, bumping impression and there were strange whining sounds but the noise was not as deafening as I had imagined it would be. Then I was suddenly tilted back in my seat, as in some terrible fairground contraption, and we were airborne. The thumping and bumping had stopped. All was smooth, and suddenly all my fears left me. Why I don't know, but once into the sky I was just not afraid any more. In fact I insisted that Don changed places with me.

'Quick,' I said, undoing my harness, 'I want to look out of the window before we get too far away.'

'I thought you didn't want to look out of the window.'

'Well, I do now. Quick, let's have a look.'

Don undid his seat-belt and wriggled over, and I got into his place. The ground was receding underneath. It was quite fantastic. There began to be a pattern of fields of all shades of green and roads and little objects that were houses, and then, quickly and disappointingly, we were into cloud and all the ground had vanished. From one extreme of being afraid I went to another and became annoyed that the cloud prevented me from seeing anything. I wished I could take off all over again and experience a second time its new, incredible visual experience.

But the rest of the flight was rather boring, and landing at Kennedy Airport was even more of a disappointment: it looked just like Heathrow. I have no idea what I expected, never having been abroad before—green Martians probably—but Kennedy certainly did not fulfil my expectations. I found that this became a familiar reaction during the following few days. I think I had expected America to be utterly different, but what struck me most were the great number of similarities with the scene back home and I was constantly being surprised by this fact.

The differences that did strike me particularly were the air-conditioning everywhere and the constant presence of Yellow Cabs which we used a lot. On my first ride in a Yellow Cab I admired very much the generous ashtray in the back, flicking ash and putting cigarette ends into it at a great rate—until I found it was really the chute you put your money in! I was fascinated, too, by trivial differences: the traffic lights being simply green and red, with no amber; the public telephones in drug stores, and, for that matter, drug stores themselves; being commanded 'Walk' or 'Don't Walk' at pedestrian crossings; and all my romantic notions of New York gained from films and television being confirmed and compounded by two simple street signs together. One said 'Madison Avenue', the other '48th Street'. That was where we were staying and, as if I was personally living in a film, I never really believed it was true.

Yet all the time—I suppose because we speak the same language—it seemed like home and yet in so many different ways was not. The time this struck us most forcibly was just after arriving at the hotel. It was early evening and after we had been shown to our room we came down again, and feeling very hungry, I said to Don: 'I could do with some tea, couldn't you?'

'Yes, that's a good idea,' he said. 'I'll get a waiter.'

I must explain here that when I say I felt like having tea, I meant the kind of tea we have in Nottingham: not just a cup of tea nor even a cup of tea with a few polite scones and biscuits, but a pot of tea, with all sorts of eatables—a plate of bread and butter, pork pie possibly, and salad, cheese, pickles and perhaps fruit cake. This (and the pork pie idea was looming particularly large when I spoke to Don) is what I had in mind as we sat down in the lounge of our hotel in Manhattan.

The waiter came and we asked for some tea. He looked a little blank.

Don repeated the order.

'You mean, like cups of tea with tea-bags?'

'No,' said Don, 'we'd like a pot of tea, please . . .'

'A *what* . . .?'

Don went on. 'A pot of tea with something to eat.'

The waiter's amazement was beyond belief. It was as if he had just heard the Third World War had broken out.

'Tea . . . to *eat*?' he said, eyebrows hitting the ceiling and making people on distant sofas and chairs look round to see what was going on.

But before Don could expand any more on his ideas of English northern tea the waiter had turned and disappeared.

'Well,' I said, 'that's it. They obviously don't serve it and that's the last we'll see of him.'

I was wrong. Within a few minutes he reappeared, and with him was someone who looked like the manager. We felt rather uneasy. But we need not have done. The manager could not have been nicer as we explained what we meant by 'Tea'. And not long afterwards the self-same waiter, all smiles, brought us a great tray with not only endless hot water, tea-bags and cups, but an incredible assortment of the most wonderful sandwiches —turkey, chicken, prawn, and accompanied by every kind of pickle and mustard imaginable. It was marvellous. They obviously *do* have tea in New York, but they don't call it that!

But before then we had had a different sort of surprise. On the way from the airport John suddenly noticed a big black car just in front of us. 'Look at that,' he said. 'Mafia Staff Car!' I nearly went under the seat. 'Mafia Staff Car?' I said, not believing it was possible. 'Shouldn't you tell the driver to keep clear?' The driver overheard and started laughing. 'It's a joke,' he explained, as I was still waiting for tommy guns to appear from the windows of the black limousine. 'Oh,' I said. 'It's just a plate anybody can buy,' he went on. 'You could buy one and take it back home and stick it on your automobile.' 'I see,' I said, feeling rather silly, and then we all had a good laugh at this first example of New York humour.

As we drove on to Manhattan Island I noticed that, although there had not been a cloud in the sky, it gradually seemed to get darker. Then I understood why. We were now driving along streets like canyons where every single building was a sky-scraper. I looked out of the window and up and up at these cliff faces of concrete and glass, and they seemed to go up and on for ever. I found it rather disturbing.

Our hotel room was on the tenth floor: not very high, perhaps, by New York standards, but certainly the highest I had ever been in a building in my life. I steeled myself to look out and down on to the street below where the traffic seemed like Dinky cars, and I felt quite remote and unconnected with the human beings I could see like specks on the pavements. I didn't like it one bit. Later, I liked even less sleeping at that height. I lay in bed and had a strange, detached mental picture of myself suspended at that height, with the roar of traffic beneath, never-ending, and me right up there with nothing to support me, lying horizontal in the air. I didn't sleep much that first night.

The next day we met Tom Congdon, our American publisher, and discussed the schedule for the week: we were to be

launched on a round of personal appearances, a lot of broad-
casts from local radio stations and one television show, the
widely-networked *Today Show*. The television was first on the
list, and as we drove down to the studio I was very aware that I
was glad I had brought Emma's lead with me. The thought
of appearing before this enormous American audience was
quite daunting. I took the lead out of my bag and carried it
into the studio with me. I felt mentally that Emma was there
trotting beside me, quietly being more confident than I was,
pulling gently on the lead and transmitting a message to me:
'It will be all right. Don't worry. Remember when we were
on the *Russell Harty Show* and I went to sleep? Think of that.
Think of me beside your chair. You'll be all right.'

I was introduced to the interviewer who, I saw, had noted the
lead dangling from my hand and I fancied that I also saw a
thinks-balloon rise swiftly from his head with a big question
mark in it.

'Er . . . I've brought Emma's lead,' I said. I thought I had
better somehow explain, but saying that only seemed to make
it worse.

He looked slightly nonplussed.

'You don't mind do you? Only . . .' And then I couldn't
really explain the true reason, and just went on lamely and
apologetically, 'You don't think it looks stupid, do you? I'll
keep it out of camera shot. No one will see it.'

He smiled as if he then really understood. 'No, go ahead . . .
feel free. It's fine.' Then he took me through the sort of questions
he would ask, the technicians came and lit me up and did their
tests, and soon I was absorbed in the business of the interview.
But all the while I kept a tight hold of the lead down in the
chair beside me, and as we were cued in and the show began, I
imagined literally that Emma was down there too, curled up
asleep, giving me confidence in the way that she always did,
and proving once again how much I still needed her.

In between fulfilling our commitments to the schedule Tom had
mapped out, we had plenty of time to look at New York. It was
such an exciting city, and vibrated and tingled with bustle and
life, and gave a strange, heightened sense of feeling good to be

alive. I had only one major, permanent disappointment. I really did expect to see Fred Astaire in top hat and tails dancing along Fifth Avenue, and when there was no sign of him I was quite sad! I suppose that was an indication of how much films influence the average English person's idea of New York. But there was a plus side to this. We were relieved that it was possible to walk about and not see gangsters in a street fight, and not be mugged at every corner, nor was there a sign of the equivalent of Kojak keeping down the crime that we have grown accustomed to think flourishes every second of the day or night in New York.

We were strolling along one evening and came across a police patrol car parked by the sidewalk. John and Don were so full of admiration they had to stop and look all round it, but just as Don was peering at the light on top of the car we saw the policeman coming towards us. I stood back, wondering if he was going to arrest us there and then, and fascinated by the gun in his holster which swung ominously as he approached. I felt I had seen this sort of thing on television, and didn't fancy being despatched to the morgue.

But what the policeman said was: 'Hi! How'd ya like it?' I think he must have guessed immediately we were English tourists.

Don leapt back from the car as if shocked by several thousand volts and looked defensive. John also managed to look shifty, although we were doing nothing and the policeman seemed friendly.

'Er . . . marvellous,' we said at last. The policeman opened the door.

'Get in,' he said.

So that was it . . . the soft approach . . . we were going to be taken for a ride to whatever Precinct Police Station . . . But before this thought had really time to materialize, the policeman followed up.

'Go on, get in. You're English aren't you? I'll take a picture of you if you like sitting in a genuine New York police car.'

And that was it. We chatted to him. He took Don's camera as we all piled inside and heard the radio crackling out messages, and he took a photo of us, then Don took one of him and me

133

smiling in front of the car. It was all so friendly, and that incident with the policeman was typical. We found the American people so marvellously warm and open. Meet an American for five minutes and you know his entire life-story. Another lovely thing we found was that complete strangers spoke to us. Quite unlike England. It is impossible to savour the true meaning of 'English reserve' and realize what a handicap it is until you have been to America. 'Have a good day,' everyone said and they really meant it. Try that on a Nottingham bus at seven in the morning, I thought.

Visiting New York radio stations was a different kind of eye-opener. Although I had found that the television studio had been very much like one of ours at the BBC or LWT back home —except it was high up in a skyscraper block—the radio stations were as unlike Broadcasting House as could be imagined. I was extremely surprised. I had expected everything in New York to be on a bigger scale, so when I went into my first radio station and found it was tucked away in a small room high up at the back of a downtown office block, I could hardly believe it. Also the people who ran them were far more informal than I had been used to at the BBC. They were all very easy-come, easy-go, and were even more advertising-minded than our own commercial stations.

One station we went to advertised nothing but kosher products. Of course, I had done a lot of interviews for commercial stations in England and was used to having the advertising slipped into the interview. But I was not quite prepared for what happened here. I was in the middle of telling them a story about Emma, and had reached a dramatic bit where Emma saved me from being knocked over and killed on a pedestrian crossing, when suddenly I was stopped. A man leaned in front of me and, without any warning, started a great harangue about the quality of kosher salad cream and then broke into a little ditty about it. When he'd finished he grinned, and I got on as best I could picking up the threads of what I'd been saying: 'Where was I? Ah yes. On the edge of the pavement. . . .'

We then went on to discuss my eye operation and I was just about to say what it was like when the bandages came off for the first time when . . . a hand on my shoulder. Stop everything.

The man was back clutching another bit of paper and broke immediately into song. Wonderful kosher butter this time.

I found it very difficult to put much enthusiasm into relating the first moments of sight when all I could think of was kosher butter.

One of the nicest radio stations we went to in Manhattan was run entirely for the blind. They broadcast about twelve hours a day, reading news headlines, a serial-extract from a book, and giving all sorts of shopping information for blind people. It was run by a blind person and I really took to the interviewer, a former actress called Judy. Of all the interviewers we met she was by far the most attentive and enthusiastically interested in not only the story of Emma and me, but also in Don and what he had to say and how he felt.

This was another aspect of American broadcasting people that made them so different from their English counterparts. Invariably they want to know far more about how you felt in any given situation. 'And what were your emotional feelings then?' seemed to be their favourite question. And, of course, to anyone English that is never a very easy question to answer. We keep ourselves to ourselves and don't regard our feelings as public property. Both Don and I found it all rather refreshing, however, and in the end we became quite good at actually saying what we felt. I thought it was rather endearing that Americans set such store by people's emotional reactions, and how they felt it was all of interest to everyone else. Perhaps it might do us English a bit of good to take that particular leaf from their book.

When we left this radio station and I had put Emma's lead—once more my mainstay—back in my bag, I had a reminder of her even more forcible than the lead could ever provide. There at the edge of the sidewalk was a guide-dog with her master. But to my horror there was, just in front of them, a begging-bowl. I was shattered.

Begging is not illegal in New York, but the blind man and his dog were somehow very different for me from all the other people we had met asking for money. I was not at all sorry for the blind man, but I was moved almost to tears by his dog. Perhaps it is a terrible way to think of it, but my reaction was that he knew precisely what he was doing and his dog did not. The poor dog had no choice but to sit and beg with her owner. It was so sad.

Apart from isolated incidents like this I was enjoying our American trip, but I thought constantly of Kerensa and Emma, wondering what they were doing, imagining Emma romping about with Buttons in the garden, and hoping that a wistful thought or so might cross her mind. I tried desperately to adjust to the time difference between New York and Nottingham, and would be walking along Fifth Avenue at lunch-time, look at my watch, and even my permanent regret at the absence of Fred Astaire would be blotted out. I would whizz the time on by five hours and think: it's Kerensa's bedtime, or: Mum will just be putting the dog food out. And my mind, superimposing the most unlikely image on the bustle of Manhattan, would picture Emma and Buttons putting their brown noses into their bowls. Having Emma's lead was a comfort, but it was no substitute and I really wanted it to work magical powers and somehow transport Emma across the Atlantic there and then.

To make up for this I made a phone call home every day. Kerensa thus knew that I had not really disappeared, and my mother told me afterwards that when these transatlantic conversations took place, Emma sat near by inclining her head very much like the dog on the gramophone record label and with an expression that said: 'I know who you're talking to, so everything's all right.'

I could not wait, in the end, to get home. The details of the flight back, saying goodbye to everyone, the final broadcast from a cramped back room have all become a blur in my mind. My only clear recollection is of us returning up the M1 motorway towards Nottingham. The first thing we'll all do, I thought, is go for our favourite walk together, Don, Kerensa, Emma, Buttons and me. We'll all go over the fields above the house where you can see for miles, and I shan't miss the first colours of autumn in the leaves. It will be marvellous and we'll be together again.

Our homecoming was unbelievable. It had been only six days since we left, yet it felt like six centuries. As we came up the drive to the house I thought: I never want to leave English

136

soil ever again. Emma came dashing out of the front door with such exuberance and excitement, with Buttons behind her wagging her tail so furiously that it bent her entire body from side to side as if in our absence she had somehow become made of rubber. Then Kerensa came running towards us giving a shriek of delight, and I think all this gave me a far greater feeling of guilt about leaving them than when I left. Perhaps it had not been such a traumatic experience for all of them as it had been for me. But certainly for weeks afterwards, every time I went to bed at night, I lay there and imagined having to leave them again. I know lots of people must go and leave their children and dogs and never really think twice about it, but I am sure that for the rest of my life I shall remember that great outburst of affection from Emma, Buttons and Kerensa as we came home, and it will remain my main reason for resolving never to leave them again.

When we had eaten our tea—a proper Nottingham tea, already laid out for us *and* including pork pie and salad and currant loaf so that we truly knew we were home—and my mother had related what news there was (mostly minor naughtinesses on Kerensa's part, but how good the dogs had been) and John had left, we went for our walk. I felt an immense contentment as we all moved along in a happy family gaggle with Kerensa holding Don's hand, chuntering (I think) 'Mummy, Daddy, back, all come back.' Emma and Buttons were on their leads sniffing once again all the good and familiar smells in the hedgerows and stopping for particularly attractive ones, so we had to keep up a chorus of 'Come on Emma . . . Buttons, come on.' I, meanwhile, was looking at the trees, which in only a week had begun to turn a little, for it was September, and I knew that in the days to come there would be even more marvellous colours to watch for.

The little lane we went along to get to the fields which spread away above the village and rolled towards the purple-coloured Derbyshire horizon, is one where local legend has it that the highwayman Dick Turpin used for his hold-ups. Whether he ever did sit on Black Bess under the very tree we were walking by at that moment and shout 'Stand and deliver!' I don't know, but it is certainly called Baulk Lane. And it was here, on the way back, that something happened to remind me that Fate rarely deals an absolutely perfect hand. I had thought perfection itself lay in that walk up to that point, but the extra card dealt by Fate, while not actually flawing the perfection, nevertheless made me think what I otherwise would not have done: I was reminded of who I was, how lucky I was now, and how things might have been so different.

Kerensa had recently made it plain to us that she would like to take a more active part in walking the dogs, and would pester us to allow her to take Emma's lead in her own little hands. Even though she was not quite two we gave in, if only for a quiet life, and at first, after a few uncertain steps, with the gentle Emma trotting obediently by her and implicitly obeying every stop-go in this strange slow progress, Kerensa had usually had enough and was satisfied. The lead would drop to the ground, Emma would stop and attend to an unsniffed patch of grass, Don or I would pick it up and on we would go.

So it was on this occasion. Kerensa decided that she wanted her turn with Emma. We had just come over the stile from the fields and were coming down into the lane where there is a pavement. Kerensa walked along behind Emma and Emma trotted sedately along, keeping that same body-length away on the left as she always did. Don was by my side, and Kerensa and Emma were just in front of us. Then I noticed something odd. Kerensa was walking along quite confidently holding the lead. But she had her eyes closed.

'Don,' I said, touching him on the arm, 'look at that.'

'What?' he asked. I motioned him to stop and pointed to Kerensa, whispering, 'Kerensa—look. Whatever is she doing?'

Don was amazed. We watched. Emma stopped to sniff at the roadside. Kerensa stopped and stood there with her eyes tightly closed. When Emma moved off, Kerensa moved too, eyes still closed.

I was astonished, and it made me remember an incident not long before at home to which I had paid little attention and certainly had not thought in any way significant. Kerensa had been playing in the living-room and I noticed she had her eyes closed and was walking towards the coffee table with arms outstretched. She had felt the coffee table and felt around for the little mug she knew was there. When she found it, she had opened her eyes. I thought it was simply a new game. 'What are you doing, Kerensa?' I had asked. But she had just giggled. Even if she'd had a more extensive vocabulary I would probably have been no wiser. I thought no more about it—until that afternoon in Baulk Lane.

Could it be just play? My mind at first refused to entertain another possibility. We continued down the lane, and Don and I didn't speak as Emma continued to lead Kerensa. How could Kerensa possibly know Emma had been a guide-dog? Obviously she could not. She had never even seen anyone work with a guide-dog. The nearest she had ever seen was a little silver statuette of a guide-dog with harness which lived on our window-ledge, but that didn't demonstrate how guide-dogs behaved. And how could she know that in closing your eyes there is simulation of blindness?

It was all very strange and disturbing, and made me think that there are forces acting on human beings of which we know very little. Could it be that the genetic code which transmits from one generation to the next the smallest detail of physical characteristics, and temperament as well, also passes on some of the parents' memory bank? What other explanation could there be? I watched, and was unnerved, and even a bit scared.

But Emma brought it all to an end by doing something she would never have done with me when I was blind and she was on harness. In sudden pursuit of an obviously irresistible scent, she walked Kerensa into a lamp-post. Very gently, I must add, but it made Kerensa open her eyes and look as if she was going to cry, then she changed her mind and dropped the lead. We were back to reality.

Apart from that strange incident, it had been a perfect September day. When we got back home after our walk I reflected how much I loved September and the beginning of autumn, and how so many good things always seemed to happen to me in September. I had got my sight back in September only three years before. And there was my birthday. For some reason I mentioned all this to Don when he came into the room after hanging up the dogs' leads.

'Ah yes,' he said, 'your birthday.' And he gave a kind of grin.

'What's so funny about my birthday?'

'Nothing,' he said, 'nothing.' He became very mysterious, and bent down quite unnecessarily to fiddle with the television set.

'Have you got my present?' I asked, more as a joke than anything.

'Well,' he said, still making a production of adjusting the set, 'you *are* asking, aren't you?'

This really did whet my appetite.

'Don,' I said, 'what have you been up to?'

'Up to? Up to? Nothing, petal, nothing at all.' And he turned and laughed, and added, 'But I haven't forgotten your birthday.'

I decided not to pursue the matter. Something was on and it was something connected with my birthday, but it was useless to ask.

Three days later the mystery was solved; I understood why he had been so secretive and I was glad I had not attempted to question him any further on the evening we had come back from America.

Don gave me the most unbelievable and fabulous birthday present I have ever had in my life.

CHAPTER TWELVE

I PASSED THE next three days in a state of pleasant anticipation. All sorts of ideas went through my mind as I was going about the house, taking Emma and Buttons for their walk, seeing to Kerensa and looking after the cats. What had Don been so mysterious for? Was I right in thinking he had got me a special present? If so, what could it be? I do not have many really ambitious ambitions, if you know what I mean. I've no desire to own the Taj Mahal, so my mind really didn't get much beyond the possibility of an outsize bottle of Chanel No. 5. Then I had an inspiration. Was this it? A china Labrador dog figure, beautifully fashioned and coloured, which we had seen a few weeks before in a shop in Nottingham . . . What about that? I had grabbed Don's arm when I had seen it and we had gone inside and inquired the price—and come out crestfallen. It had been marked at nearly a hundred pounds! Not counting VAT! 'Never mind,' Don had said sympathetically, as we gave it a last, longing look in the shop window. 'Some things are not meant.'

The more I thought about the china dog, the more I was convinced I was on the right track. I dusted the coffee table down and pictured what had happened. Don had gone back and bought it for me secretly. That was it. I knew. I began thinking where I would put it. We have quite a collection of china dogs, but this was the most beautiful I had ever seen and would deserve pride of place. I played the fascinating mental game of shifting all our other pieces to accommodate it. I shall know immediately I get downstairs on my birthday, I thought, because he always puts the presents with the cards on the hall table, and I shall know by the size and shape however much he has tried to disguise it in wrapping-paper.

But when the day arrived, what happened?

Nothing.

There was nothing at all in view as I came downstairs. True, there was a pile of cards on the hall table. But beside them—empty space.

Ah well, I should never have looked forward so much, never built my hopes up. But I didn't give up hope entirely. Don had already said 'Happy Birthday' to me, and I thought that perhaps he was saving it for breakfast-time.

But breakfast-time came and went and it was just like any other breakfast, except that I looked at my cards: a lovely one from Don, one in his writing on behalf of Kerensa, and cards from my family and some friends. I didn't want to say 'What about my present, then?' because that would have sounded terrible, and anyway I knew Don had not forgotten.

Then he came into the house at mid-morning from the surgery for his coffee, he stood there in his white coat and grinned at me again with his special enigmatic air. He sipped his coffee and said: 'How do you fancy a trip in the car this afternoon?'

'A trip in the car?' I asked. 'What do you mean, Don? Where to?'

His grin grew broader. 'Well, ask no questions—but do you want to come for a trip?'

So that was it. He had ordered the china Labrador, but hadn't picked it up. That was where he wanted to take me. I didn't ask any more questions. I just laughed and said, 'All right.'

We set off—minus Kerensa and the dogs for some reason he had insisted on—and turned out of the drive towards Nottingham. The china dog occupied my thoughts. Then instead of going straight on at the first roundabout, which would take us into Nottingham, he carried on turning and went off in the direction of Derbyshire. Now I was mystified. Don had a strange satisfied and expectant look on his face. I decided to let things happen, and not ask any questions at all.

Soon we came to the junction with the M1 motorway. Don, quite silent, turned on to it, and began driving north. Where *could* we possibly be going? And why? On we drove, past one junction, then another, for miles. Then at last he began to slow down. The big blue signpost pointed off the M1 to Alfreton, and here he turned off.

By now I was quite lost and had no idea what we were doing in the streets of this little Derbyshire town. Don, however, seemed to know what he was up to, and as we waited at some traffic lights he grinned, looking more than ever like a Cheshire Cat, and said, 'Won't be long now.' Eventually we pulled up at a house on the outskirts of Alfreton. A pleasant-looking woman came to the door. I was now in such a complete state of puzzlement that I was no longer capable of being surprised.

'Hello, Mrs Hall,' said Don.

Mrs Hall? I thought. Mrs Hall? That sounds familiar— what do I know about Mrs Hall?

Then the penny began to drop.

Before we had gone to America we had been watching Emma and Buttons playing. I had thought that Buttons, being a year old, would soon be coming into season and that had led us on to thinking how nice it would be to have little chocolate-coloured Labrador puppies.

Emma had been spayed, as is the normal practice for future guide-dogs, and therefore had never been able to have puppies. But it seemed that via Buttons we might find a way of giving her a family by proxy, so to speak. I had then remembered that there was someone reasonably local who bred chocolate-coloured Labradors, and had done so since before the war. It occurred to me that they might have a chocolate-coloured stud dog. So Don and I looked them up in the Yellow Pages, and there they were, name of Hall, with an Alfreton number. But when I rang to inquire if they had a stud dog the line was engaged and, with all the preparations for going to America, I had put the idea to the back of my mind and not done anything more about it. As I stood on Mrs Hall's threshold all became clear. I may have set the matter aside, but Don had not.

Mrs Hall was very pleased to see us. She had read the book and knew all about Emma. 'In fact,' she said, 'I bought it because of the chocolate Labrador on the cover. There aren't many about, you know.'

I said I realized that, and told her about Buttons and the way we had got her.

'Oh, you were very lucky,' she said. 'Well, as I told your husband on the phone, I haven't got a chocolate stud dog at present. But the litter I told him about is here all safe and sound—and I've saved the chocolate-coloured dog for you in case you want him. The rest of the chocolates have been taken, and all the others are black.'

So I still had not unravelled the mystery. No china Labrador and now no big chocolate-coloured stud Labrador . . . what then? My mind was in a whirl. A chocolate-coloured puppy! That really must be it . . . third guess lucky. I looked at Don. His face was all delight at my reaction. I was lost for words.

Mrs Hall smiled too and said, 'If you come with me, we'll go and have a look. It's such a nice day I've put them out on the lawn.'

We went outside and there they were: a heap of what looked like plain and milk chocolate-coloured dogs, with some liquorice ones, surrounding a contented-looking mum.

'Which is the dog among the chocolate-coloured ones?' I asked. Mrs Hall picked him out for me. 'Here he is,' she said, and handed me a small, wriggling, bright-eyed little bundle.

'Oh, aren't you beautiful!' I said, taking hold of him. He was just like the picture I had of Emma at two weeks old.

Don looked at him with as much admiration as I did. 'Isn't he lovely? I wish Buttons had been a puppy but, of course, we've never seen any advertised.'

'No,' said Mrs Hall, 'I don't think you will. Chocolate Labradors are getting very popular now, but it's been a long, hard struggle. We've been breeding them since the nineteen-thirties, and originally no one wanted to know very much. The demand was all for yellows and blacks. In fact, I think some breeders put chocolate Labradors down!'

I was horrified. I couldn't believe her. I was really upset at the idea and held the small bundle closer to me. The idea of having any puppy put down was bad enough, but chocolate Labradors . . . I thought of little Emma and I wanted to weep.

'Yes,' said Mrs Hall. 'It's terrible, but they wouldn't do it now. We've got a waiting-list, and we're not the only ones.'

I returned the little puppy back to his family where he immediately tunnelled under several brothers and sisters, determined to get back to mum.

Don, still all smiles and plainly radiant with delight at the surprise, said, 'What do you think, then?'

I didn't know what to say. The puppy was so lovely and cuddly and so reminded me of what Emma must have been like—though I had never known her then, and had seen only photographs—it was almost heart-breaking. But there were so many considerations. We had talked about breeding 'little Emmas' as an idea, but without really going into practical details. This all tied in with our ambition to buy a big kennels. Yet we had not discussed what Emma might think and how she might react to yet another addition to the family, and a tiny one at that. I thought Don had been wonderful arranging this as a birthday treat . . . and yet . . . I felt I could not take a decision there and then. I was torn in two. Nevertheless, I was sure it would not be fair if we said on the spot that we would take this little dog without really going into all the implications.

'I think he's lovely, really lovely,' I said at last, 'and I think it's the most wonderful birthday present I could ever have. But don't you think we ought to give it twenty-four hours before we decide, Don? I really do want him. But we've got Emma to think about. Would Mrs Hall let us ring her tomorrow, and then we shan't be letting her down if she's got another good home for him to go to.'

Even as I said it, I hated the thought of this little puppy going anywhere but back to join Emma and Buttons. Furthermore, while I had been standing there I'd had an inspiration. It had come to me that the little puppy's colour was exactly that of the bracken which by the autumn is so browned and burnished in the sun. I thought he ought to be called 'Bracken'.

But we had to be sensible, and I explained everything to Mrs Hall.

She readily agreed to our idea, but added, 'You won't keep me waiting too long, will you? Because there are one or two others very keen on having him.'

We promised we would let her know by the next day at the very latest.

'If we do decide to take him,' I asked, 'when would we be able to pick him up?'

I imagined Mrs Hall would name a date in about a month or so, but she said, 'When he's six weeks old . . . in about three weeks' time.'

I was rather surprised it was so soon but I didn't say anything, and Mrs Hall had the final word.

'If you do decide to have him,' she said, 'you'll promise me one thing, won't you?'

'What's that?' I asked, wondering what was coming.

Mrs Hall laughed. 'I was most disappointed that you didn't bring Emma with you today. I so wanted to see her, having read so much about her. If you do come again to pick up the new one, you will bring Emma as well, won't you?'

We all laughed.

'Of course,' I said. 'In any case, it's Emma who will have the last word!'

We got into the car and set off for home. I turned to Don. 'Well, all I can say is thanks again, petal. But you've no idea what went through my mind. I *knew* you'd fixed something up, but I hadn't the faintest inkling that that's what it would turn out to be.'

Don looked very happy. 'Well, I wanted it to be a surprise.'

'It certainly was that.'

Then, more seriously, Don said, 'But what do you think? I knew we couldn't decide then, but I had to reserve the puppy in case—because I didn't want to miss the opportunity.'

'I know,' I said. 'But what it all boils down to, I suppose, and what we most don't want to do is to upset Emma. She took to Buttons immediately, but then Buttons was more grown-up and the same sex. What would she think about an energetic little bundle who would get under her feet and wouldn't even be house-trained? I don't know.'

'No,' said Don, 'Emma's made great pals with Buttons and obviously gets on with her, but Emma still comes first. The trouble is there's no way of telling how she would get on with a puppy unless we tried it for real. It's not like those book offers where they let you have it for a fortnight on approval, send-no-money-unless-satisfied kind of thing.'

I thought about this as we went south down the motorway. Don had given me an idea.

'I'm not so sure,' I said at last. 'What about this: Mrs Hall says she's got a waiting-list for chocolate Labradors. If we took Bracken . . . the puppy that is—I think he ought to be called Bracken whatever happens, he's such a gorgeous colour—I'm sure Mrs Hall would understand if it turned out that Emma couldn't stand him, and she would have no trouble at all in finding someone else who wanted him.'

'That's true,' said Don. 'And if we had to, we could go back to our first idea of finding an older stud dog to mate with Buttons, because, after all, the only point of it all is to bring some new little Emmas along.'

I agreed, and we decided to ring Mrs Hall as soon as we got back.

She listened to our plan and, to our relief, said she had no objection. After we had made arrangements to pick up Bracken in three weeks' time, towards the end of October, she again had the final word:

'Don't forget to bring Emma, will you? I'm really only making an exception because of her!'

While this was going on, Emma was on her settee and Buttons was on the hearthrug. 'Little do you know,' I said, 'you two are going to have a very small brother, and, Emma, I do hope you like him because we're depending on you.'

Buttons carried on sleeping, but Emma opened an eye and gazed up rather quizzically with a look that suggested: 'I know there's something afoot. I don't know what. But this sort of thing is nothing new. I'll wait for it to happen.' And she closed the eye and went to sleep again.

The prospect of having little Bracken made me very happy. I was somehow confident that Emma, who had shown she was by no means set in her ways when Buttons had arrived on the scene, would also get on with Bracken. Only one other slight problem seemed to be on the horizon. I was still a bit perturbed about taking Bracken at only six weeks. They were still only babies at that age. Somehow I had it in my mind that the minimum age for puppies to leave their mums for the outside world was eight weeks at the very least. Yet I knew Mrs Hall was experienced, and trusted her.

It was a happy coincidence, then, that about a fortnight later

I happened to meet Derek Freeman. Derek is in charge of puppy-walking and of the puppy-breeding scheme for Guide-Dogs. I met him when I was lucky enough to be shown round Tollgate House near Leamington Spa, which is the centre for these activities. Derek knew more about dogs, about whelping, rearing and training than anyone I had ever met. If you showed him the pedigree of any Labrador he could tell you about any dog on the chart.

He showed me a litter of puppies who were about to go and be puppy-walked, which is an essential stage of training for future guide-dogs.

'How old are they?' I asked.

'Six weeks,' he said. 'They always go out to be puppy-walked at six weeks.'

Once again I was amazed.

'Isn't that rather young?'

'No, no, not at all. We've tried all sorts of different ages, and we've found that if they go out at six weeks they settle better with their puppy-walker, they learn to be house-clean and they're socialized that much earlier. It's the ideal age. You've got to remember that up to this age these dogs have been living in a litter in a kennel, and the sooner they can get out and have individual attention and training the better they're going to be. We really have had much more success with puppies going out at six weeks than at any other time.

Then I told him about our plans for breeding, our ambitions for having our own kennels, and about Bracken, and my reaction to collecting him at the age of six weeks.

'Well,' said Derek, 'that breeder's quite right. You mark my words. You'll train your puppy very easily if you have him at that age and he'll be house-clean in no time at all.'

I told him that it was by no means certain that we would be able to keep Bracken when we got him, and that it all depended on Emma.

Derek laughed. 'I know how you feel,' he said, 'but don't cross your bridges till you come to them. I shouldn't worry.'

So, when the big day arrived for us to go back to Alfreton and collect Bracken, my mind was quite at rest on this score. This time we all went: Kerensa, Emma, Buttons, as well as

Don and myself. I felt that with yet another dog we should soon need a bus rather than a car.

We got to Mrs Hall's. She was thrilled to see Emma and liked the look of Buttons, and let them both out on to her lawn where they proceeded to take no further interest in the business of collecting an addition to their family. Then she brought Bracken to us, and he looked even more lovely than when we had first seen him. He was bigger and his coat seemed richer than ever in colour. Kerensa squealed with delight and wanted to hold him, and, true to form, danced up and down, saying, 'Mummy, Mummy, *another* Emma!'

And, with Bracken on my lap, and Emma and Buttons taking only the mildest of interests, this strange caravanserai made its way back. If that's how the other two are going to treat him, I thought, he'll just have to stay. We had agreed with Mrs Hall that we would give it a fortnight to see how things worked.

But we need never have worried. All Derek Freeman's assurances came true. Bracken was house-trained within the two weeks, and Emma and Buttons, though appearing disdainful at first, soon accepted him in his place—as a puppy.

At first Emma quite ignored him. She pretended that he simply did not exist. Bracken, in turn, would rush up to Emma thinking she was his mum, scrabble with his paws, and stretch up to try and lick her nose. Emma would back away in disgust and, mustering as much dignity as possible, retire to her sacred place on the settee. Bracken stood there not quite sure what to do next. Then he would spot Buttons. Ah, a more likely target! He would rush up to her, legs like india-rubber. Buttons was rather more welcoming and obviously, quite early, took a decision that this must be *her* puppy. She took charge of him and guided him off to her basket where he sat and nuzzled her.

The living-room now, when all three were there together with Kerensa, presented a bizarre sight. Kerensa, perhaps, would be surveying the world from her potty, surrounded by wall-to-wall chocolate Labradors!

A lovely relationship grew up first between Bracken and Buttons, and then, as she got used to him, a different but equally lovely relationship was apparent between Bracken and Emma. By the time our fortnight's 'trial' was over it was certain that Bracken was a permanent addition to the family, and I was so relieved and happy when I felt the moment had come to ring and tell Mrs Hall that all was well.

Bracken was such an intelligent puppy. By the time he was eight weeks old, he was not only house-trained, but was learning to sit and to come when you called him. It was obvious that he would not be long in being able to respond to the basic commands, and Derek Freeman's prophecy that he would be easy to train was proving right. He was one of those puppies that it is a pleasure to own, and with every day Emma became more interested in him. I felt very soon, in fact, that despite the early apparent indifference on Emma's part, she and Bracken were very close. It is very difficult to describe, but I felt—and the impression has grown since—that Bracken had some sort of connection with Emma. It was an elusive sort of notion that somehow came to me out of Bracken's activities and the way that Emma began to play with him even more than she did with Buttons. At the same time it was evident that Bracken had a deep respect for Emma.

Emma continues to sleep in our bedroom as she has always done, with her bed at the foot of ours. Buttons and Bracken had their baskets in the kitchen. But from very early days with Bracken, the mornings were enlivened by a new and quite delightful ritual, with a daily never-failing sight that Don and I still think so lovely. As I am cooking the breakfast, Emma comes downstairs and puts her nose round the kitchen door, and this is the signal for Bracken and Buttons to do homage to her. Bracken is always first, Buttons following him. Bracken rushes up to Emma and washes her face with sheer delight at seeing her. He barks with excitement and whines with joy as he rushes, slipping on the lino, to tell her how much he has missed her. Emma is pleased to see him, too. She stands there in the corner of the kitchen, wagging her tail quietly as she allows him to lick her face. Then, suddenly, that's that. She lets out one sharp—but not angry—bark that indicates: 'That's enough, young man, that's enough!' Bracken leaps back, always astonished, flattens himself to the floor, and looks at her with an adoration that suggests he would happily steal the Crown Jewels just for her. Buttons is a little bit more ladylike, but she too cannot resist making a big fuss of Emma, although in a quieter manner. She sniffs affectionately and wags her tail while Bracken is bridling his exuberance, still barking and wagging his tail but not daring to do otherwise because from those earliest days he knew that Emma's word is canine law.

The special something that I felt in connection with Bracken and Emma came out in all Bracken's deeds. He had been in the garden one morning and when he came in he brought with him a rose-bush, roots, soil and all, but with his soft retriever's mouth apparently quite untouched and unharmed by thorns.

'Bracken!' I exclaimed, 'where did you get that from?' He wagged his tail happily, growled and started to chew this marvellous prize.

I rushed out into the garden. There was an enormous hole, and, strangely enough, Emma was sitting by it.

'Who did that?' I said to her. She looked up at me with great innocence and then rather pointedly at Bracken as he came charging out of the kitchen still with the rose-bush in his mouth, looking like a small canine version of the bit in *Macbeth* where they carry Birnam Wood about the stage. Emma continued to look at him, and if her paw could have been an accusing one she would undoubtedly have pointed it.

'Well, *he* did it,' her look suggested. 'He did it, of course.'

'Yes, but who told him to?' I said.

Emma blinked at me and turned the other way. But although her back was most expressive and non-committal, I *knew* who had instructed Bracken, and why.

When Emma was a puppy, one of her favourite tricks had been digging up plants in the garden. Paddy Wansborough, her puppy-walker, had told me that. 'I planted a hundred bulbs one morning,' she had told me. 'A hundred. It took me hours and hours, and I let Emma into the garden—she wasn't very old—just for a run round, you know. Then I wondered why she hadn't come in, and when I went to the door you would never believe it! Every single bulb I'd planted, crocuses, daffodils, tulips, you name them, Emma had dug up and carefully put on the back doorstep. There was an enormous pile of bulbs on the step and Emma, very pleased with herself, wagging her tail beside them. I knew she meant it all as a huge gift, so I couldn't blame her, but it *was* annoying.'

So here was I, fourteen years later, doing exactly what Paddy Wansborough had done. I stood looking at Emma.

'Emma,' I said, 'I'm sure you told him to do that.' She opened her mouth and grinned at me, pushing her tongue out as Bracken leapt round the garden with his prize.

'Oh well,' I said, 'I suppose if you did it as a puppy, we can expect him to.'

I went back indoors and told Don what had happened. It was as if an electric shock had passed through him. 'Dug up one of my rose-bushes? He hasn't!' And he rushed out into the garden. 'Bad dog!' he yelled. I followed him. 'Don't shout at him,' I said. 'Emma did that as a puppy.' Don turned, surprised. 'Oh? Did she?' Yes,' I said, 'don't you remember Paddy Wansborough telling us?'

'So she did,' said Don, and then, all annoyance gone, he called to Bracken who was doing his best to see that the rose-bush would never bear any roses. 'Come on Bracken, drop it.' He turned to me. 'I'll have a go at planting it again.'

And re-plant the bush he did. Not that it did much good, because fifteen minutes later Bracken was back with it again in the kitchen.

It was quite uncanny, but this was only one of the occasions when Bracken repeated what Paddy had told me Emma did as a puppy. He was fascinated by the television. Emma apparently sat for hours as a puppy and watched television. He loved the plants in the garden, and even more, he loved to chew them up. 'Emma when she was little was certainly no angel,' Paddy had told me.

I know it sounds far-fetched, but I feel there is a part of Emma in Bracken and that somehow he is a continuation of her. I mentioned this to Don. 'Do you think that's silly?' I asked.

'No,' he said, 'I know what you mean. But I know why you like it particularly. Bracken's a puppy and does all the things that Paddy told you Emma did. You never had Emma as a puppy and couldn't have seen her, and so now it's lovely to see what she was really like.'

152

A day or two after the incident with Bracken and the rose-bush, Don reminded me that it was November the Fifth the following weekend. My mind immediately went back years: Guy Fawkes Night, the smell of bonfires in the damp, chilly air, and, even though I had not been able to see them, the whoosh of rockets and cracklings in the sky.

'One of the patients was telling me they're having a big bonfire up the road,' Don said. 'Do you think Kerensa's old enough to appreciate some little fireworks if we keep her well away? Not bangers and that sort of thing, but the pretty ones, you know . . .'

'Well,' I said, 'I'm sure she would, and she's old enough to hold a sparkler anyway. But in any case *I* wouldn't mind having some fireworks myself.'

Don's eyes lit up—almost like Roman candles.

'Would you really?'

'Well, wouldn't you? Be honest!' I laughed. 'I bet you're itching to go and get some rockets and dying to let them off.'

Don laughed as well. 'Ah . . . now you come to mention it, I wouldn't mind at all.'

So that afternoon we all went off into Long Eaton where we knew there would be a better selection of fireworks than locally. But alas for our foresight. We had forgotten that Wednesday was early-closing in Long Eaton.

'Would you credit it?' Don said as we arrived in the market-place. 'All the firework shops are closed.'

'Well, there might just be somewhere open. Let's try up here.'

We went up another shopping street.

'It doesn't look very promising,' said Don as we got out of the car and went up the street. Kerensa took Emma's lead. But we were no luckier.

'It doesn't look as if there are any firework shops up here,' I said.

'No,' said Don, 'but there's a pet-shop open over there. Look.'

And, sure enough, a strange bright oasis in a desert of unlit shop windows, there was a pet-shop. Even if we got no fireworks, I thought, Emma will think the journey worthwhile.

We crossed the street and looked in the shop window. It was

Kerensa who first spotted something unusual—something, though we had no idea at the time, which was about to become a part of our home-life. Temporarily, I'm thankful to say.

'Birdie,' said Kerensa. 'Look Daddy. Birdie.'

'Oh yes,' Don said, 'look at that green bird there. I wonder what kind it is?'

'I don't know,' I said. 'I'm not really very up on birds, but it looks something like a parrot.'

'Mm. Isn't it handsome?' said Don. 'I've always fancied having a parrot, you know.'

I was astonished. This was something he had never mentioned to me. I laughed. 'Well, learn something new every day. You never told me.'

'Yes,' he said, 'always had a fancy to own a parrot.' He looked at me, quite seriously. 'Shall we go in and have a look?'

'If you like,' I said, rather dubiously.

We went into the shop. Emma and I and Kerensa browsed round the shelves while Don hung his nose over the cage with the green bird in it. When we got back to him he was deep in conversation with an assistant.

'No,' she was saying, 'it's not a parrot. It's a parakeet.'

'Ah,' said Don, obviously not well-versed in the differences between parrots and parakeets. The assistant went on: 'He's very nice. He's only five months old.'

'Oh. How big will he grow?'

'He'll never be much bigger than he is now.'

'They do talk, don't they?'

'Oh yes, they talk like mad. They'll say absolutely anything. Especially that one.'

I stood by silently watching this exchange, and noted that if this parakeet was going to be such a good talker he was obviously a late developer as he moved silently on his perch. But Don did not seem to draw the same conclusions.

'How much is he?'

'We've reduced him. Only twelve pounds.'

'What's he been reduced for?' asked Don, becoming wary for the first time.

'Oh, because we've only got *him* for sale and there's no choice,' said the assistant. She said it all too promptly for my liking and her logic totally evaded me, but Don seemed almost satisfied.

'There's nothing wrong with him, then?'

'No, nothing at all. He's a very good buy at that price.'

Don's doubts were dispelled, and I didn't interfere although I privately thought that if you have always had a mad urge to own a parrot or parakeet it does not encourage sales resistance.

Don looked over at me. 'What do you think, petal? Have we room for a parakeet as well?'

'Well, I suppose one more creature more or less isn't going to make much difference.' I laughed and added, 'Don't tell Ming, though.'

'Ah, I hadn't thought of Ming.' Then after a moment's thought: 'I suppose we could take him out of the room when Ming came in, and vice-versa?'

'We could,' I said. 'But Don, I'm a bit frightened of birds— well that sort anyway. You'll have to look after him.'

'They don't take any looking after at all, birds don't,' he said, by now taking his wallet out. And, with a strange gleam in his eye, he said: 'And we'll have him talking in no time!'

So we didn't come home with a box of fireworks. Instead we had a parakeet in a cage which Don carried triumphantly into the house. He was like a man suddenly obsessed. He decided he would call this newest arrival Captain Flint, and I imagined him setting out for the pub like something out of *Treasure Island*. Kerensa was also thrilled and sat by the cage for the rest of the day pointing and announcing, 'Birdie.' But I am afraid that I, and, it later transpired, Emma, did not share their boundless enthusiasm for Captain Flint. It was the start of a not very beautiful friendship.

CHAPTER THIRTEEN

WE DID MANAGE to buy some fireworks the following day. There was no time to go back to Long Eaton, so I did the rounds of the local shops and, despite leaving it late, came back with an exciting, brightly-coloured assortment. Don gazed approvingly, and picked each one up, examining it with a gleam of anticipation: Roman Candles, Golden Showers, Giant Catherine Wheels, a Mount Vesuvius and a Mount Etna (these turned out, disappointingly, to be different only in name), Silver Fountains, Peacock Tails, Bengal Lights, and plenty of sparklers and rockets which, alone, had helped to eat up most of the remainder of the housekeeping money; but no Thunder-flashes, Jumping Crackers, Jack-in-the-Boxes, or those terrible aerial whizzbangs that make Bonfire Night more like a version of trench warfare in your very own back garden.

Kerensa was fascinated and thought (as she did about so many things) they all looked very edible. 'Sweeties,' she said, jumping up and down to get a better look. Although we tried to explain, before putting all the fireworks on a high shelf in the kitchen out of reach, that they were certainly not for eating, there were the inevitable tears, and we resigned ourselves to having to make more explanations before Saturday night.

Captain Flint, by now, was installed in his cage by the window, and gazed out morosely, jigging about on his perch. Don went through the box of fireworks and occasionally turned to him to say: 'Pieces of Eight, eh Captain? Pieces of Eight?'

I was astonished at the way this bird had suddenly intruded on our lives. In less than twenty-four hours he had added his own dimension. 'What do you mean, Don? "Pieces of Eight"?' I said.

'Well, you know,' he said, 'it's treasure. He'll learn to say it if I keep on.' He turned to the cage again. 'Pieces of Eight!

156

Pieces of Eight!' The bird took no notice but this didn't deter Don, who, between the fireworks and his new acquisition, seemed somehow to have suddenly reverted to his schooldays.

'Don,' I said, 'it sounds ridiculous.'

'No, no,' he persisted, laughing. 'He's got to learn, and all parrots—I mean parakeets—ought to know "Pieces of Eight". Shouldn't they Jim Laaa-ad. . .?'

'Well, make up your mind. Which is he, Captain Flint or Jim Lad? You'll confuse him.'

'Never,' said Don, 'never. He's an intelligent bird is that . . . aren't you Cap'n?'

I thought, well you could fool me, but said nothing.

When Don turned to go back to the surgery I could have sworn there was a slight wooden-legged roll in his walk, and I imagined for a moment I saw a three-cornered hat perched on his head. Whatever had come over him?

Would Captain Flint somehow take possession of Don? I hoped not. Some men raced pigeons in their spare time, collected stamps or tinkered with motor cars, and these I could have put up with, but having a parakeet as a rival was something different. I also hoped it would not prevent him from organizing the firework party. We invited Harold, Betty and their dog Zelda down for the weekend to help with the celebrations.

They arrived on Friday, and we set about preparations for the next evening. Don, although not entirely ignoring Captain Flint, concentrated on his side of the organization such as collecting wood for the bonfire, and doing the rounds of the shops for the food and drink.

'Sheila, are you going to make some bonfire toffee?' Betty asked me.

'Oh,' I said, 'I suppose we ought to, to go with the baked potatoes.'

It was something I had forgotten about, one of the traditional things about November the Fifth, and as soon as Betty mentioned it I remembered that years ago, before I was married, we used to have firework parties and that I still had a recipe for bonfire toffee written out in braille. I told Betty, and went to rummage among the cupboards upstairs where I knew it would be—somewhere. At last I discovered it among my files of braille now happily long unused and getting rather musty. I brought it down.

'Here it is,' I said, handing it to her.

'It's no good giving it to me,' Betty laughed. 'You'll have to do the reading—although I'll help with the cooking!'

'Of course,' I said, 'I'm sorry.' I had forgotten once again that people who have always been sighted usually have no idea how to translate the raised patterns of dots that make up the braille alphabet. I began to run my fingers over the brown sheet of paper. It was more difficult than I had anticipated. But not because I had forgotten braille.

'It's a long time since I made this recipe,' I said, 'but I must have used it quite a bit. The dots are nearly worn down into the paper.'

At last I began to make sense of the recipe, and I started to laugh.

'What's funny about bonfire toffee?' Betty said.

'It's not the recipe, it's what happened when we made bonfire toffee one year. I've just remembered.'

My mind was already back in 1968, when Emma and I were sharing the little flat in Peel Street, in the middle of Nottingham, with my great friend Anita. She and I had first met when I went to evening classes for writers. At the time, I was trying to improve my stories and she was writing a novel. The flat was in a large, rather decayed Victorian house and the furniture was nothing very grand, to say the least. But it was home and I was happy there, partly because Anita was very practical and helped me enormously, but also very much because she never allowed me to think that I differed in any way from people in the sighted world.

Anita had bought some fireworks for November the Fifth, and she had really done it very much for me: a good illustration of her attitude to me as a blind person. I, however, thought she had taken leave of her senses.

'Anita,' I said, 'fireworks don't mean a thing to me.'

'Oh, they will, they will,' she said in her no-nonsense Hull accent. 'I'll have a little bonfire out the back, and the smell's gorgeous, you know that, and I'll be able to tell you all about the colours and the marvellous patterns the fireworks make. You'll enjoy it, you really will. And we'll make some bonfire toffee, although we'll have to get a recipe for that from somewhere.'

I had agreed, with reservations. Not that there would have been much point in objecting because Anita, once set on a course, was well nigh unstoppable.

When we got back from work the following evening, Anita set about making the toffee. I had found someone in my office who knew how to make it and had put the recipe into braille, and I read it to Anita who, in turn, had copied it down.

But I heard her getting exasperated as she stood at the stove and I couldn't understand why, because the smell was quite delicious. 'Sheila,' she said at last, 'are you sure you haven't left anything out of this recipe?'

'No, positive I haven't.'

'Well, it's terrible. It won't set. It's all sloshy.'

I heard further sighs and groans, accompanied by mysterious shaking sounds of the saucepan on the stove. Finally Anita said, 'It's a pity we haven't a fridge, then we could freeze it into setting.'

'I don't think you're meant to do that.'

More sighs. 'Well it doesn't look at all tempting. It's no good, we'll have to give it up. Let's get on with the fireworks.'

I heard her clanking about with the saucepan and what sounded like a tin tray.

'What are you going to do with it?' I asked.

'I'm putting it to cool on a tin under the sink,' she said, 'and it looks more like glue than toffee. I'll get rid of it later.'

So we went out with our box of fireworks. Emma wanted to come out as well, but I knew that November the Fifth is not the favourite date in a dog's diary. They hate the bangs and get frightened, so we left her inside.

'We'd better pull the outside door to,' said Anita, 'otherwise Emma might get out.'

'OK,' I said.

Next I heard her putting a match to the little bonfire she had

159

built and soon I could smell the fabulous scent of the smoke, hear the hiss and crackle of the wood burning and feel on my face the heat of the flames.

'I think we'll have a Catherine Wheel first,' she said.

'Is that the one that goes round and round on fire?'

'That's the one.'

'Can I feel it before you start?' Anita handed me the firework and I felt the round coil and the bit in the middle with the hole in it, so I knew what it looked like.

I heard her knocking a nail into the fence. Then there was a hissing and a whirling and whizzing sound. 'It's beautiful,' said Anita, 'like a dragon's tail on fire going round and round, all jagged yellow, with fabulous circles of blue and red spinning in the middle.'

I could picture the Catherine Wheel perfectly. Then, when it had died away, Anita said, 'Roman Candle next . . . it's an incredible green light, lighting up all the garden, and with great clouds of smoke . . . hope the neighbours don't mind . . .' I could smell the gunpowder and it was wonderful. 'Now it's turning red . . . now white . . . it's dazzling.' Finally there was a popping sound. 'And that's that. Just a little ball of flame gone into the air.'

And so it went on. Anita described it all vividly and I thought that if her novel was as good it would be worth reading. It didn't matter that I couldn't see anything: I could even visualize the sky over the garden because, whenever there was a crackling or explosion high up above, Anita would tell me about whatever rocket had gone fizzing up. 'There's another one . . . it's a burst of white, like somebody throwing a whole handful of diamonds into the night and then losing them . . .'

At last all our fireworks had gone and we turned to go back inside. I gave a push at the door. Nothing happened.

'It's locked,' I said. 'Did you put the catch down?'

'No. At least I don't think I did. Let me try.'

I heard her banging at the door.

'It's no good,' she said, 'and I haven't got my key. Have you got yours?'

'No,' I said, with a feeling of apprehension, to say nothing of cold, coming over me.

'We'd better ring the bell. There's bound to be someone in the house.'

But although we rang and rang the bell, no one came.

'What idiots we are,' said Anita as we stood there shivering.

'We?' I said.

'Well . . . me then!'

'I'm a bit worried about Emma,' I said. 'She'll think we've deserted her. Can you see her through the letter-box?'

I heard the clink of the letter-box being opened.

'Yes,' said Anita, 'she's all right. I can only see her tail end, but she's in the kitchen.'

'I'll call her,' I said. I bent down and called 'Emma . . . Emma!' But I heard no response, no click of paws up the hall.

Anita had a look. 'She's still in the kitchen. She's not taking any notice.'

We both called as loudly as we could. It must have been a weird and slightly disturbing sight for anyone passing by, two grown people bent double against a door and shouting 'Emma' through a letter-box.

Still nothing happened.

'Whatever is she doing?'

'I don't know,' said Anita. She was silent for a moment, then, slightly aghast, she added, 'But I think I've got an idea . . .' Then, as if suddenly possessed, Anita started shouting at the top of her voice: 'Emma . . . *no* . . . naughty dog . . . *no* . . . *leave it!*'

I was quite alarmed. 'What's going on?'

Anita took no notice of me and carried on shouting: 'Bad dog . . . *Emma* . . . *leave it!*'

'Leave what?' I asked.

Anita paused briefly and turned to me.

'The toffee!'

'Oh no!'

'Oh yes! And she's not taking a bit of notice. She'll be as sick as a . . . sick as a dog.'

'Oh, poor Emma,' I said.

'Poor Emma—what do you mean?'

'That horrible toffee . . .'

'It wasn't as horrible as all that.'

'Well, it won't do her any good. Let me try and stop her.'

161

So I bent down and shouted. But it had no effect. I could now hear from inside the flat a clanking sound on the floor. I knew immediately what that was. Emma must have finished every last scrap of toffee, and was now pushing the tin round the kitchen.

What an end to our firework celebrations! Well, perhaps not quite the end. The couple who lived upstairs eventually came home and let us in, and by that time Emma was fast asleep, snoring, and stretched out on the kitchen floor like a Roman after an eating orgy for one. Beside her was the tin. Empty. Not only that, but in order to get at some toffee stuck to the outside she had thoroughly chewed the edge thereby rendering the tin fit only for the dustbin, where its contents should have gone anyway.

She was not sick, but paid in another way for her folly. She had terrible indigestion, or at least I think that is what it must have been. Called to her dinner the following day (an event which usually brought her bounding to the bowl) she took only a mouthful or two before retiring for further sleep. Anita reported that she had looked very guilty and had been munching grass rather thoughtfully in the garden.

I suppose that even the cleverest of dogs have their faults, and Greed had always been Emma's one and only Deadly Sin. This time, however, she seemed to have hit the jackpot. But one good thing came out of it all. She was cured for life of any further interest whatsoever in toffee.

So much so that when I told Betty the story and we eventually began making our toffee, Emma, who had been lying quite happily with us in the kitchen, suddenly twitched her nose tentatively, got to her feet looking strangely shifty and reminiscent, and made quietly for the door. As she went, I thought (although it could have been imagination) that it was the first time I had ever seen a chocolate Labrador start to go green at the gills.

And that evening, Harold, who had not heard the story, innocently offered her a lump of our product, which had turned out this time to be excellent. Emma sniffed it once, and with a 'No! Not again!' expression backed away and again left the room.

The party went marvellously. Harold and Don had a

splendid time letting the fireworks off in the garden, while Betty and I 'ooh'd' and 'aah'd' with Kerensa dancing about behind the safety of the dining-room window. At the same time, with the ascent of the first rocket, Bracken, Buttons and Zelda, led by Emma, took themselves off with much dignity and disdain to another room until it was all over.

After Guy Fawkes Night, and Harold and Betty gone back to Yorkshire, life settled back into its normal pattern. Well, almost. Don was now able to concentrate more of his attention on Captain Flint. Yet the more he persisted with trying to teach him 'Pieces of Eight', the more the wretched bird remained stolidly non-cooperative, and silent except for raucous screeches which he never emitted, for some reason, when Don was in the room.

It became increasingly evident that Emma had not taken at all to this strange green thing which bounced unnervingly up and down in its cage. More than that, I soon realized that Emma positively disliked Captain Flint. I suppose the reason that it took me some time was that I have never known Emma to dislike anything (except of course bonfire toffee and, when she was very young, passing cats). So I was not familiar with the symptoms.

It was not that Captain Flint screeched a lot, but when he did the din was ear-splitting. And I came to realize that he screeched at precisely five-past two every weekday afternoon. Now this was the time that Don had just gone back to the surgery (after spending his lunch-time saying 'Pieces of Eight' in between mouthfuls), Kerensa had been put in her cot upstairs, and I always had what had been until then a pleasant quiet ten minutes sitting on the settee with Emma before getting on with my work.

It was our special daily ten minutes together. But now, no sooner had I sat down than the Captain turned on his perch, gave a preliminary jog or two, gazed balefully out over the room, and started screeching. Immediately, Emma got down from the settee and, tail between her legs, left the room en route for her bed upstairs. I thought it odd, but decided that she just didn't like the unusual noise (and who could blame her?) and that in time she would get used to it.

Then I noticed that in the evening, instead of taking her usual place on the settee, she would sleep on the floor near the door. The parakeet never uttered even the quietest squawk in the evening. Nevertheless, Emma invariably kept one eye open, and that was a wary one directed at the cage. I think it took me nearly a fortnight to realize that it was not simply Captain Flint's noise that Emma disliked. She hated him altogether.

And her reactions got worse before I realized that. Instead of simply climbing resignedly off the settee in the afternoon and going quietly upstairs, she would now make a bolt for the door at the first screech and gallop upstairs, sometimes not coming down again until nearly four o'clock when her face would appear rather nervously round the door with a look that said: 'Is it safe? Has that terrible thing shut up?'

'Don,' I said one evening, aware that he might be upset, 'I don't think Emma likes the bird.'

'Doesn't like the bird? Why, Emma doesn't dislike anything. What makes you think that?'

'Well, she doesn't like it when he screeches. In fact, she's terrified. She flies upstairs to her bed when he does it and I can't get her down.'

'She doesn't look frightened to me.'

'I know, but she's not in her usual place on the settee, is she? That's near the bird-cage. She's near the door. See if *you* can get her on the settee.'

'Come on Emma, old girl,' said Don, 'up on the settee.'

Emma looked up at Don, then at the bird, and stayed firmly where she was.

'It must be some sort of phase she's going through,' said Don obstinately, and turned to the bird-cage. 'Come on, Cap'n, Pieces of Eight . . .' The bird stared back at him without the slightest flicker of interest in his beady little eyes.

It took me some days to convince Don that it was not a 'phase' that Emma was going through, because he was never there to see poor Emma do her Great Escape Act. It was as if that evil parakeet was really a terrible bully (and therefore a coward as well) and waited till Don was out of the way before terrifying Emma and deriving from it all a sadistic pleasure.

At last things came to a head. Emma would no longer even

come into the room where the bird was, and stayed out in the hall most of the time.

'He's got to go,' I said to Don.

He looked quite startled. 'Who?'

'Captain Flint. I'm sorry, but that's it.'

'Why?' said Don. 'He's a lovely bird. Come on Captain, Pieces of Eight, Pieces of Eight . . .'

'I'm sorry, petal,' I said. 'I know he's your parakeet, but Emma really is frightened to death of him. He's making her life a misery, and I think she's beginning to wonder whether this is really her home.'

'Are you sure?'

'Positive. I just wish you could see it. And hear it for that matter.'

'Hear what?' asked Don.

'Well that's just it. He screeches like a banshee. But he never does it when you're here. Emma hates it. I tell you what. Tomorrow, you can go out after lunch as if you're going back to the surgery as usual. But instead stay in the hall. The bird will think you've gone. Then you can see what happens—that is if I can get Emma to cooperate and even come into the room and on to her settee.'

Don looked concerned. 'Well, all right,' he said. 'It seems a bit of a charade but I don't want Emma upset at any price. I'm sure that the Captain doesn't mean it.'

'No, maybe he doesn't,' I said soothingly. But I was sure I knew Captain Flint better than that.

The next afternoon Don pretended to go out as usual, even to the point of giving me a kiss and saying 'See you at tea-time, petal.' But he stayed just outside the door. Kerensa had been put to bed and I had managed to coax Emma, against her better judgement, to come and sit with me on the settee. The moment Don had disappeared, the Captain opened up with the most appalling squawking. Emma leapt off the settee and almost left smoke-trails as she rounded the door and galloped upstairs. Then Don re-appeared, rather like a demon king in a panto-mime, at which point the Captain shut up as quickly as he started and squirmed about on his perch obviously thinking that since he had wings he might be mistaken for an angel.

But it was no good. Don was astounded. 'Well,' he kept saying, 'well . . . I would never have believed it. What a terrible noise. Poor Emma! You're quite right petal. He'll have to go.'

And go he did, and that was the end of Captain Flint. Fortunately, I had a friend who had made the mistake of saying that if we ever parted with him, she would love to have a parakeet. Little did she know. But she had no dog that he could torment, and I thought this the best way out.

After the Captain had gone, cage and all, Emma quickly got back to her old, civilized routine. It took her a little time to adjust to the fact that there was no malevolent little eye trained on her as soon as she came into the room. At first, she looked rather cautiously round the door before venturing further, and you could almost see a look of relief when she saw there was no cage and evil green occupant. Then she came in as briskly as she always had before, got up on the settee and, once again, we were able to enjoy our daily special ten minutes together.

In the evenings there was peace again, and I myself found I had to get used to the silence being broken only by Emma snoring beside me, and no jingling sounds from the cage in the window. In fact I had to say to Don: 'I think you'll have to go back to saying "Pieces of Eight."'

'Why's that?' he asked.

'Well, now you're not saying it all the time, I think you've fallen asleep.'

We both laughed, and Emma woke up and joined in the fun, sneezing and wagging her tail because she knew we were all a united family once again. Not for the first time I realized what a special relationship I had with Emma. I loved the two younger dogs, but it did not occur with them. I was still very close to Emma. Now that I could see, some of the communication between us which used to transmit itself through the harness had gone, perhaps because it was no longer needed. But I still knew exactly what she wanted, and she knew exactly what I wanted without my having to speak a word.

I didn't have this sort of relationship with Buttons and Bracken, and, somehow, was rather surprised, and certainly missed it. With Bracken, in particular, when I started training him for obedience, I felt he should know so much because Emma had always known so much. I only ever had to show Emma something once and she would immediately know what to do.

I had always relied on Emma, not simply to guide me when I couldn't see, but to take the lead in other ways. Bracken, of course, would not do that. He looked to me almost in the way I used to look to Emma, and that is something I had never envisaged before having a dog other than Emma. Bracken expected me to do everything, to show him everything, and I had to train him in a very different way from that which I had imagined. I had to keep telling myself that he was a dog, and I was a person, and I had to train him every step of the way without expecting that he would intuitively do things for me. It took me a long time to change my attitude so I could work with an ordinary dog. Not that I consider Bracken just any ordinary dog. He is very intelligent. But, each in their own way, both he and Buttons managed to demonstrate what an extraordinary dog Emma was and is.

Emma is a very self-contained dog, and if she were human, which she very nearly is (as well as having far nicer attitudes than most of the human race), I feel she would be a Victorian lady with a strict moral outlook. Often she will sit on the settee and look at me, or the other dogs, with such a distant look on her face, containing not quite disapproval but certainly a measure of appraisal. If Buttons or Bracken comes up to her and she has no desire to speak to them she simply ignores them. She turns her back, tucks her nose under her paws, and that's it. Emma's final word.

Emma was, of course, trained as a guide-dog before we actually met. Nevertheless, it was up to me to keep up her standard of training. But with Emma, this was so easy. I remember once wanting to teach her scent. In case I dropped something I wanted her to be able to find it because it had my scent on it, and I wanted her to ignore things with other people's scent. I had a vague idea how to do this, and I knew that I could not use articles in the house as, even if they were not specifically mine, they might have my scent on them. So I explained to the girls at work one morning what I wanted to do.

'I want to teach Emma scent,' I told them, 'so if I put my purse on the floor, can you each put down something of yours.' They rummaged in their handbags, and each put something on the floor. I gave Emma my hand to sniff and said, 'Go on Emma, find my purse.' So off she went, and immediately picked out my purse and brought it back to me.

I was very pleased, but thought: Well, that's my purse, and it probably has a very strong scent so we'll try something else. So we each put down an envelope, and one of the girls marked mine with a pen. We put the envelopes around the floor of the office at various scattered points, and Emma was sent off again. She came back to me with one, and touched my hand with it. 'Has she got the right one?' I asked. The girls told me she had, the one with the mark on it. We tried this at intervals over several days, and every time Emma unfailingly returned to me with the right envelope. Either she had learnt immediately and simply knew straight away what was wanted, or the whole thing was a series of coincidences—and that I refused to believe.

But it was not until I started training Bracken that I realized the true extent of Emma's exceptional accomplishment. He (and other dog-owners confirmed the experience) took a long time to acquire the skill. I was told that it was difficult to teach a dog to use his nose. But because of Emma, I had not believed them!

Another miraculous ability of Emma's was the way she would not have to be told more than once about a new route we were taking. I took it all for granted at the time, but now I know it was something quite out of the ordinary. Other dogs are just not like Emma, or vice versa. No wonder I accepted and treated Emma as another person, someone I could explain my problems to, someone on whom I could rely, and who was my best friend in the entire world.

Training the other two dogs, with Bracken always the more responsive, took up the rest of the year after Captain Flint had faded into the memory like a bad, green dream. Our life through that winter and into the spring became a very pleasant routine of runs in the park and over the fields for training, with Emma coming for exercise as well, and Kerensa, now growing apace, more and more confident as she held Emma's lead. I was also looking after my own cats, doing the rounds of cat shows and seeing to the various Siamese that came to stay in the cattery. It was a full and happy life.

Then, out of the blue, came a marvellous surprise. I had a telephone call from Mrs Pauling. She and her husband were breeders of Labradors, and it was they who had owned Emma's father. They had read our book and were thrilled and delighted at Emma's achievements and fame. They wanted us all to go and visit them up at Cookridge Farm not far from Leeds, in Yorkshire. But it was not simply an invitation to go out for a day. We were to go to a Labrador Rally! Now there was something to look forward to. When I announced the news, three chocolate-coloured faces looked up happily and three tails wagged, as if the significance was very well understood. What a prospect!

CHAPTER FOURTEEN

THERE WAS AN added attraction to the Labrador Rally apart from meeting Mr and Mrs Pauling who had owned Emma's father. They had also invited Colonel Clay of the *Yorkshire Post* and his wife. It was they who had bred Emma and given her to Paddy Wansborough to become a guide-dog. I was really looking forward to meeting them as well as to the general idea of a Labrador Rally. It was a gorgeous Sunday morning as we set off for Leeds. By now, with Bracken nearly nine months old and Kerensa growing all the time, the back seat was so crowded with dogs and the front seats with humans that the population density of the car would have caught the eye of any housing inspector on the look out for slum clearance.

'What happens, incidentally, at a Labrador Rally?' Don said as we drove along.

'I've no idea,' I said. 'I think it's just a fun-day for Labradors, and possibly their owners.'

From Leeds, we turned out of the city on to the Tadcaster road and emerged into open country. 'Which way, now?' asked Don.

'Well,' I said, making the best sense I could of the map, but looking in vain for Cookridge Farm, 'Mrs Pauling said that it was on "the top road", but I can't see any top road, or bottom road for that matter.'

We ploughed on. Don was looking a bit worried. 'What did she actually say?' he asked.

I laughed. 'Well, she kept saying: "It's on the top road. You can't miss it." I asked her how we should know which was the top road and she sounded very surprised. All she said was, "Well, there's only one top road, you'll have no trouble."'

'I see,' said Don, slowing down to examine a signpost. 'Well, that's not it. Do you suppose we're on the top road?'

'I really don't know. The map's no help at all.'

By this time we were practically into Tadcaster, and, top road or not, we had certainly missed the unmissable Cookridge Farm. We turned back and after half an hour of U-turns and sudden halts to look at tiny side-lanes, we found it.

And what a sight greeted us. A field with a line of parked cars, shooting-brakes and Land-Rovers—and, it seemed, all the Labradors in the world, mostly yellow and black, in what I can only describe as a happy state of flux, dashing here and there, wagging happily, making friends, and, some of them, lying contentedly and well-behaved beside picnic rugs. We parked, opened the back doors, and out came our chocolate-coloured contribution to the throng. Emma, Buttons and Bracken emerged one by one, shook themselves, then, looking about them, could hardly believe their brown eyes. An entire land-scape of dogs! Unbelievable. It was as if they had landed on another planet, the planet of Labradors! Whoopee! They took off all together into the middle distance, and I was left standing by the car holding three leads in my hand. 'I don't think it matters,' said Don. 'They all seem to be off the lead anyway.'

They were back in a surprisingly short while, however, having done a rapid tour of inspection, and stood panting and wagging their tails happily, with Emma, despite her years, not the least excited of them.

The man in the next car looked across. 'Excuse me,' he said, 'that wouldn't be Emma, would it?'

'Yes, that's right,' I said.

'Well, would you believe it? I've read the book. You'll be Mrs Hocken then.' He came across, bent down to pat Emma and held out his hand. 'Pleased to meet you. I've had Labradors all my life, but I don't think I've ever had one as clever as yours.' He bent down and patted Emma again as she lay on the grass, tongue out, her tail wagging. 'What a good girl.'

And that turned out to be the pattern of the entire day.

Don and I met no one we knew, but everyone seemed to know us—or to be more accurate, everyone seemed to know Emma. 'What's going on over there?' said Don. 'Come on Kerensa, let's have a look.'

'Want to take Emma for a walk,' she said.

'No, come on, Emma's having a good time on her own.'

Some sort of trial seemed to be going on in one corner of the field. Dummies were being shot over the fence, and dogs were going and fetching them back.

'I wonder if we could have a go?' I said.

'Why not?' said Don, and we went to speak to a man waiting his turn with a black Labrador. The man explained: 'It's a working test. The judge assesses your dog for working ability. Has your dog done anything like it before?'

'No, but I'm sure Bracken is game for anything. What do you have to do?'

'Well, they throw these dummy bags over the fence . . .' (the dummy bags looked like rolled-up pieces of cloth), 'and you have three separate tests: one where your dog just jumps over the fence and retrieves it, then they hide it in the bracken and he fetches it back, and then they put it among the trees to see if he can find it.'

'Shall we enter Bracken?' I said to Don.

'Do you think he's good enough yet at retrieving?'

'Well, he fetches his dumb-bell back but I don't know what he'll think about one of those dummies.'

'The judge'll let you use a dumb-bell,' said the other competitor, 'after all it's only a bit of fun. Get your dog entered and see what happens.'

'Go on,' said Don, 'put him in for it. I'll look after Kerensa and the other two.'

So Bracken was entered, and with Don shouting, 'Go on Bracken young lad, show them what you're made of,' Bracken stalked with me up the field, head high, knowing that something important was going to happen.

'Has he done anything like this before?' asked the judge.

'No, but he does go to training classes and he will retrieve, although so far he only retrieves a dumb-bell.'

'I've got a dumb-bell in the car,' she said with a kindly smile. 'We use that and see how he does.' She went to fetch the dumb-bell and at last it was Bracken's turn.

'You start here,' said the judge. 'That gives your dog a twenty-yard run, then he's got to jump that fence where the markers are and find the dumb-bell in the long grass.'

'Fine,' I said.

Kerensa and friends

(*above and opposite*) Sheila and Kerensa out walking with the dogs

Don, Kerensa,
Sheila with (*from
left*) Bracken,
Buttons, Emma

'Now don't let him go until we tell you. We'll throw the bell, and then I'll tell you to let your dog go.'

I looked down at Bracken. 'Sit, Bracken. Now wait and watch them throw the dumb-bell and you've got to jump over the fence and get it back.' Bracken looked back at me with wisdom far beyond his age, as if he knew all about it.

'Right, send your dog!' called the judge.

'Off you go, Bracken,' I said.

Bracken shot up the field like a bullet. I was so proud. Look at him, I thought, he's never done it before, but he's going to show all these older dogs how it really ought to be done. I could see the judge with a pleasant smile on her face and obviously thinking, Here's my winning dog. She turned to me. 'How old did you say he was?' 'Nearly nine months,' I said, trying not to sound boastful.

Just as I was speaking, Bracken reached the fence, and just as in my mind's eye I saw him flying over it, he came to a screeching halt and stood there stock still.

'Bracken,' I called, aghast. 'No. Fetch your dumb-bell.'

He looked round uncertainly, tail down.

'Go and stand at the fence,' said the judge. 'Go and pat the top of it.'

Bracken watched as I did this, then put his nose down in the grass and went scenting off along the fence.

'I know,' said the judge. 'Climb over the fence and stand in the other field, then he'll come over.'

I climbed over the fence. Bracken looked up for a moment, and then went back to an obviously very delicious scent.

'Run the other way,' said the judge. 'Run down the field. Make him think you're leaving him.'

'Bracken,' I shouted, starting to run. 'Bracken!'

Bracken immediately began to bark in terror. His message was quite plain: 'Don't leave me, don't leave me.' I went back to the fence. Poor Bracken, he was most upset. 'He's not going to jump it,' I said to the judge. 'Never mind, it was worth a try.'

'No,' she said, 'don't give up.' She called a steward and I could see them chatting.

Then, to my amazement, the steward came and lifted

Bracken over the fence. I thought I was dreaming. 'There,' said the steward, 'now fetch your dumb-bell.' I could hardly stop laughing. 'I bet that's the first time you've ever lifted a gun-dog over a fence,' I said. He grinned. And Bracken recovered quickly, rushed into the grass, and picked his dumb-bell up.

Honour was satisfied, even if the rules had been bent; but, apart from not feeling able to stand the strain of running, jumping and climbing fences, I thought it would be pushing our luck to carry on—and I didn't want the steward to risk serious injury by having to lift Bracken over again. So we withdrew, and Don almost burst his sides when we got back and told him about our adventures. 'Well,' he said, 'it's a good job we didn't buy you for a gun-dog, Bracken old lad. Never mind, you had a good time.'

We walked over to the far corner of the field where we had not been, and, to our delight, there were some other chocolate-coloured Labradors. Kerensa was thrilled: 'Mummy . . . more Emmas, look!'

Then I heard a voice say, 'Hello . . . are you Emma?'

'Yes,' I said automatically, 'that is, no—that's Emma there.'

It was Mrs Pauling, who had invited us. We shook hands and introduced ourselves.

'How marvellous to meet you,' I said. 'You bred Emma's father.'

'That's right. But doesn't Emma look well? How old is she now?'

'She'll be sixteen this year,' Don said.

'Well, isn't she wonderful. And don't you look like your Dad!' Emma wagged her tail appreciatively. 'Come and meet my husband,' said Mrs Pauling, 'and see the photographs in the house.'

She led us out of the field to their beautiful farmhouse. On the way we paused at their kennels which were full of Cookridge Labradors, and I am sure both Don and I were thinking the same thing: 'One day, we'll have our *own* kennels.'

In the house, Mrs Pauling took us straight to a big picture on the wall.

'There,' she said, 'there's Emma's father.' Then she turned.

'And that's her grandmother.' It was incredible: like going to a country house and suddenly discovering for the first time rows and rows of portraits of your own ancestors staring down. The family resemblance was quite uncanny, and I felt so proud on Emma's behalf. She just followed us around and looked strangely possessive among all the pictures, a little affectionate brown figure following us, looking up as if she really *knew*, and wagging her tail gently at each frequent mention of her name.

We learnt that Emma had true aristocratic blood in her veins. Her aunt, Cookridge Tango, was the first chocolate Labrador in the country to be a champion, and her forebears had won a great many prizes in their time. It was marvellous to talk to Mr and Mrs Pauling. Like Mrs Hall, from whom Bracken came, they had been among the first breeders in the country to be really interested in chocolate Labradors, and they, in turn, obviously felt very proud of their connection with Emma.

Throughout the day Labrador owners came up just to talk to Emma, just to give her a pat and to say, perhaps, that they had called their dog after her or had bought a chocolate because they had so liked the book and her picture. It was wonderful to feel that Emma had done so much for chocolate-coloured Labradors and to think that people had actually named their dogs because she existed. 'Of course,' was someone's comment, 'mine hasn't done the things Emma's done, but at least she's a little like her with the same colour and the same name.'

Later that afternoon, I heard another voice behind me: 'Look . . . it's my dear Emma.' This was Mrs Clay, with Colonel Clay, who actually bred Emma before donating her as a guide-dog. This was another tremendous thrill. Mrs Clay bent down to Emma. 'You look so well. To think you were that little puppy we raised and you've done so much and now you're so famous!' I listened and, as always, felt quite humble at the way people spoke to Emma. 'Now,' said Mrs Clay, opening her handbag, 'I've brought you a picture of Emma's mother.' It was lovely, and I thanked her.

'She does look a bit like her mum, doesn't she?' said Mrs Clay.

175

I agreed, and said, 'I've found out the pedigree of her father's side from Mr Pauling, but I wondered if you would have her mother's side?'

'I'm sure we've got it somewhere.'

'I'm just interested,' I said. 'I'd just like to have Emma's pedigree. Not, I suppose, that it matters what sort of a pedigree a dog like Emma has.'

'No,' said Mrs Clay, turning to her husband. 'We never did have another puppy like her, did we?'

This all helped to set the seal on a wonderful day. It was amazing to have found, at last, such evidence of Emma's ancestry, and we talked about it in the car on the way home. Meanwhile, in the back, Emma had suddenly become rather duchess-like and wore an expression that plainly said: 'I don't know why you're so surprised. I could have told you I'm out of the very top drawer.'

CHAPTER FIFTEEN

EVEN BACK IN the days when she was guiding me, people worshipped Emma; but it is different now she is famous, and another illustration of how life changed after I could see. But, although it is now four years since I had the eye operation, the feeling of needing Emma has never quite left me. I still do not like going out without her, and I also like to reserve times when just Emma and I, and not even Kerensa, go out and do the shopping. Then it is like the old days, and I think Emma enjoys it so much, and we feel almost like one again even though connected through a lead and not a guide-dog harness. But going along the street is a bit like a royal procession, and sometimes I feel, quite without resentment, that I know what it must be like to be married to a famous film star. 'Morning Emma,' is always the first greeting, then, 'Morning, Mrs Hocken.' But as well as those who really have known Emma for years there are, as a result of the book, some who claim acquaintanceship from way back.

One day I was in the park with the dogs when I noticed that everywhere we went we seemed to be followed by a little old lady bustling along with a Cairn. I was in a hurry that day because I had a talk to give that evening and had somehow got behind schedule. Then, rather to my dismay, the old lady caught us up at the gate as we were leaving and confronted me.

'Is that Emma?' she said, pointing to Buttons.

Oh dear, I thought, this is going to be a long drawn-out conversation and I really haven't time. But I don't want to hurt her feelings.

'Emma?' I said, 'No, it's not Emma.' Emma was actually sniffing a bush a few yards away. But I felt a bit guilty because I knew I was somehow misleading her.

'Oh,' she said. 'I could have sworn it was Emma.' She peered more closely at me. 'But aren't you Mrs Hockridge?'

This time I had no guilt about my reply.

'No, I'm afraid I'm not,' I said, wanting very much to laugh but not daring, and not wanting to be unkind.

'Oh,' said the old lady, 'well that is funny. I know them very well, you know. Know Mrs Hockridge very well—and Emma.' At this stage, Emma, who had rejoined us, pricked up her ears and nearly gave the game away by looking interested and wagging her tail gently. Fortunately she was not seen. We managed to get away as the old lady went in the opposite direction saying to her Cairn, 'I could have sworn that was Mrs Hockridge—and Emma!'

Sometimes I look round the room at home when all the dogs are there and think how marvellous it is to see them all. But particularly Emma. The light shines off her coat, her velvet ears and wet nose, and when she sleeps, paws twitching occasionally as she dreams dog-dreams, she still looks very young, and I think, This is how it must have been for all those years when I couldn't see her.

When I was blind at least I had some idea of how she greeted people, and this was confirmed when at last I saw her, gently nuzzling a knee, never bouncing exuberantly. Emma likes affection, but she has always been a very self-contained dog. Only I have ever been allowed to put my arms round her and even then it has always been under protest, as if to say: 'Well all right, if you must, you must. But you know I don't very much like this sort of thing.' She likes to be spoken to, perhaps be stroked, have her ears fondled or a rub under the chin, but nothing too extravagant. After I could see, I realized how much she really did dislike too much fuss.

Of course, just as all human beings are different, so are chocolate Labradors. While Emma prefers her cushion on the settee and her comfort, the other two are confined to the carpet and do not mind. Emma is quite a little dog but Buttons is a big Labrador, a bit fat despite all the exercise because she is even greedier than Emma, if that is possible. She stretches right out in front of the fire, head flat on the floor, hind legs straight out behind her. But Bracken likes to tuck himself away, which seems a trait in some of the breed. You have to look for Bracken in a room, and you find him curled into a tight ball in some corner;

or, more disastrously, at the foot of the stairs where his colour blends so well with the rug that people have seen him only at the last moment as they descended, and only just averted the sort of scene Laurel and Hardy were good at.

So I look at them all, and, even with a symphony of snoring going on, there is utter peace and contentment while Kerensa is upstairs in her cot, and Don and I read or watch the television.

Emma, Buttons and Bracken behave very differently, even when asleep; and they have different temperaments. Yet it is strange how people who do not properly know Labradors lump them all together as a breed and still manage to misread their general characteristics. The impression given by Labradors is that they are easy-going with everybody, and seem ready to go off with anyone who will give them a good meal or a bed. But it is not until you have had an Emma or a Buttons that you realize that this is simply a front, an outside show.

When Buttons came to us at one year old she seemed the essence of friendliness. The very first day we got her we were able to let her off the lead in the fields with Emma, and had no problem at all in getting her to come back when called. We therefore thought she had instantly taken to us, and that was that. But Buttons was really very reserved. Whenever we came into the house, at first, she would only make a little fuss of us. She didn't take to strangers. Not only that, she could be disobedient and refuse to listen to commands. In fact, it took Buttons a whole year to be actually our dog, to be really pleased when we came in and to make a fuss of other people again.

I think Labradors are very sensitive underneath. They take life as it comes, and they make the best of things as they find them. They will not pine if they have to change homes as Buttons did when beyond the young puppy stage, yet they hold themselves back mentally until they are absolutely certain that their world has stopped changing, that they are going to stay with you, that you really love them and are going to give them a home for ever.

Bracken, having come to us at six weeks, had never known another home, and he was absolutely mine from the moment we walked into the house with him. His is a most expressive face. You can tell immediately what he is thinking and he, most of all, makes me wish I had seen Emma when she was younger. Emma would always come and touch me gently with her nose when she wanted anything in the days when I was blind, and I could hear her paws as she padded about or jumped around. But I do wish I could have seen some of her expressions that would have told me so much better than touch or sound what she was thinking and doing and, more important, what she wanted.

How much Emma has meant to me, how much pleasure she has brought and still brings! Today that pleasure is redoubled when I see her happy with Bracken and Buttons, her two companions who have helped to give her a new life in her retirement. With them in the park, instead of walking sedately from tree to tree as she would have done before they joined the family, and probably ignoring other dogs, Emma investigates with a sense of excitement, rootles round, finds exciting smells, and exchanges gossip in dog terms with the other two. If another dog comes up, all three go to greet him and play. It is so lovely.

Yet, sadly, and partly because of our runs in the park, I know that Emma cannot hear as well as she used to, nor see as well. The park is a wonderful place for dogs: not laid out with flower beds, or stifling and artificial with no sense of freedom like some parks. Instead it has great stretches of natural grass, great wild expanses with trees, and you would never think that man had designed it. But because there are such acres of space I have to be careful about Emma. Sometimes I know that she has lost me, and I have to go up to her and just touch her and say, 'This way, Emma.' I know that she cannot see very far now, although she can still definitely see. I suppose she is rather like me. Despite getting sight, my vision is far from perfect, particularly at a distance. Once something gets out of view, then it has gone. I am not complaining, I am merely saying that I think I understand how Emma's sight is now, and that is where Bracken comes in: Bracken who worships Emma, and seems to take it as his responsibility to look after her.

We were in the park one day, and, as usual, because a main road runs close by, I had walked up the path a little way before letting the dogs off their leads. After being unclipped, Bracken and Buttons normally dash off, and, in quicker time than it takes to write this, are just brown specks on a green background. Emma takes things more quietly at first. She sniffs at a favourite post, perhaps, or a tussock of grass where there is always, it seems, a scent of which she will never tire, a kind of canine equivalent of Chanel No. 5. And this is what she did on this particular occasion.

'Come on Emma,' I said, walking on with the leads and leaving her happily with her nose to the grass. Ten seconds later I looked round, and there was no Emma! She had vanished. 'Emma,' I called, 'Emma!' I looked in the other direction. There were Bracken and Buttons enjoying themselves, but Emma had not gone to join them. I started walking back along the path, calling her. I wondered if she had gone into the bushes that were close by the gate. 'Emma,' I called again, by now a little desperately, despite myself. The gate was not all that far away. And the main road. What if she had taken it into her head to . . . it did not bear thinking about. Yet, just as a drowning man is said to see his entire life, I visualized it all in a few appalling seconds, and heard the brakes and the squeal of tyres of the car that Emma would not be able to hear . . .

I really began to shout and rushed towards the gate. 'Emma . . . Emma.' At this point, Bracken came lolloping up, thinking I was calling him. 'Bracken,' I said, rather breathlessly, 'where's Emma?' He stared at me, wagging his tail, looking intent, puzzled, yet obviously working it all out. 'Find Emma, Bracken,' I said, 'find Emma.' Then at that instant I really did think I saw Emma disappearing out of the gate. 'Emma,' I shrieked at the top of my voice, 'come back!' But Bracken was already on his way and disappearing outside the gate.

A moment later he re-appeared—with Emma!

They came up to me. 'Emma, where *have* you been! You silly girl.' No anger in my voice, simply sheer relief. Emma pushed her nose against my legs and wagged her tail. 'You lost me,' I said, 'where were you going? You must *never* do that again.'

Bracken, in turn, came up, snorting and prancing with excitement. I gave him an enormous pat. 'Clever dog, Bracken, clever boy. You *knew* where she'd gone.'

As I put them all back on their leads I was never more thankful that we had brought a little chocolate puppy home to live with Emma.

Emma is now in her sixteenth year, and I suppose most Labradors live until they are eleven or twelve. I am pleased to say, though, that she is still physically fit. She has not gone grey at the muzzle, and she hardly ever ails from anything. Of course, apart from when she has a little romp with the other two, she has slowed down a lot. She doesn't bark so much when people come to the door. She still enjoys her walks, and I get great enjoyment out of being able to take her.

But I know she is getting deafer, and I have to raise my voice to her or go up and touch her so she knows I am talking to her. I also know she is going blind, which is another reason why Bracken had to go and rescue her in the park. And, with what seems a terrible irony, I know she has cataracts. It doesn't seem to worry her, however. She finds her way about and never walks into anything. It probably worries only me. Yet now, at least, after all those wonderful years of looking after me, I can give back something to Emma and look after her.

I try not to keep thinking about her age. But invariably I am reminded if I go out to do a talk, or a radio programme, or meet new people. They always ask, 'How old is Emma?' And when I tell them they start to look all sad, and say, 'Oh dear, she is getting on, isn't she?'

'Oh, I don't know,' I usually reply, 'I've heard of Labradors living till they are twenty-seven!'

I wish people would not insist on talking about her age, or be so insensitive. 'You'll not know what to do when she's gone,' they say. No, I shall not know what to do, but I hate people reminding me of it. I don't have to say that I wish she could live for ever.

I just pray that when Emma has to go, then it is quickly, and probably in her sleep, and I think about that every night when I get into bed because I lie there listening to her breathing and it reassures me, and then I can go to sleep peacefully. But when I wake up in the morning I listen again. She used to be out of her bed with a brisk shake as soon as we got up, but she often stays there now, sometimes till past breakfast-time. But I always go to her bed and touch her, just to make sure that she is all right.

There is something else I am going to have to face soon, and that is the decision not to take Emma with me when we go out giving talks. I loathe the idea. I feel able to tell people so much about her when she is actually there for them to see. Not only that, she, rather than the talk, is always the main attraction.

Only recently, visiting a local ladies' group, I looked down and saw Emma curled up by my feet. It was her usual place. But I could see she was tired and bored with the whole business, and wished she was at home on the settee. I resolved there and then that that was the last time I would ever take her. But a few evenings later, having made this decision, I was preparing to go out for a talk, putting on my coat and picking up my hand-bag from the hall-stand—but not her lead—and there was Emma sitting by the front door. She was looking at me with an expression that said, 'Well, all right you're going again. It's all very wearing for me, and I don't like the idea much. But you just *can't* leave me behind.'

And her lovely brown eyes pleaded successfully against the better judgement of both of us.

These days, more and more, I am thankful that she has the other two for companions. All my doubts, first about Buttons, then about Bracken, are long ago dispelled. Bracken in parti-cular. He looks after Emma, not only when we are out walking but he guards her at other times too, especially when all three are having their dinner.

Buttons and Emma (still) could beat any dog into eating a bowl of food. If I did not make them sit and wait for the food to be put on the kitchen floor, I would be knocked flying in the rush. Bracken, by contrast, thinks about his food. He looks at it, probably walks round the bowl sniffing and inspecting, and he may decide to eat or he may decide to wait. But he always protects Emma's dinner—and not because he covets it for himself. Emma will still be eating, while Buttons has usually finished first. In between them is Bracken. If Buttons dares to take as much as a pace in the direction of Emma's bowl, Bracken will go for her—and quite fiercely. So, greedy Buttons has to watch as Emma finishes every last mouthful under the protection of her young admirer.

Don and I sometimes look at all three of them eating their meals. Kerensa will be in the kitchen too, giving a helping—but more often hindering—hand, as, for example, when she decides an entire packet of cornflakes all over the floor will be a good supplement to the dogs' diet. At the same time, Ming has probably come out of her room and is on the watch for scraps. It is a time when I think how much has happened since that day that little Emma bounded into my life and helped to change it.

We think about the future. Our great dream remains to buy our kennels and cattery, and now it seems that it is more than mere hope, although still in the future. But before that, there is something else to look forward to.

We bought Bracken originally so that he and Buttons would produce chocolate-coloured puppies that would ensure Emma, so to speak, lived on. Buttons came into season in August of last year, and they were mated. Shortly afterwards we took her to the vet, and he confirmed what we suspected. She was pregnant.

'Yes,' he said, 'when do you expect the litter?'

'About the middle of October,' Don said.

I felt as proud as if I were going to be a mum all over again. And the timing was part of my excitement. Right in the middle of October, on the 16th, would be Emma's birthday. I hoped that Fate and Nature would join forces and help to produce Buttons' puppies on that very day!

Then Emma could be doubly proud of the new arrivals. There would be a family of puppies like her. Yet, of course, not exactly like her. For there can really never be another Emma.